The MACAT Library
世界思想宝库钥匙丛书

解析贾雷德·M.戴蒙德

《大崩溃：社会如何选择兴亡》

AN ANALYSIS OF

JARED M. DIAMOND'S

COLLAPSE

How Societies Choose to Fail or Survive

Rodolfo Maggio ◎ 著

刘露 ◎ 译

上海外语教育出版社
SHANGHAI FOREIGN LANGUAGE EDUCATION PRESS

目　录

CONTENTS

引 言

要 点

- 贾雷德·M.戴蒙德是一位博学家*，在他感兴趣的诸多领域积累了深厚的知识。他的著作涉猎多个兴趣领域，辅之以平易近人的写作风格。戴蒙德的研究方法令其享誉世界，但也使其颇受争议。

- 《大崩溃：社会如何选择兴亡》于2005年出版，该书提出了社会衰亡的五大因素；作者认为，当今世界许多社会也将崩溃，除非它们从过去的幸存社会案例中汲取经验。

- 《大崩溃》一书探讨全球的环境问题，总结人类历史的一般规律，并引起了学界的讨论，因而意义重大。

贾雷德·M.戴蒙德其人

《大崩溃：社会如何选择兴亡》（副标题亦作：社会如何选择成败）的作者贾雷德·M.戴蒙德1937年出生于马萨诸塞州波士顿。其双亲均为东欧犹太人血统，父亲是儿科医师，母亲是教师兼钢琴演奏家。戴蒙德自幼便求知欲强，因而涉猎多种领域。比如，他在剑桥大学攻读胆囊膜生物物理学*和生理学*博士学位（生物物理学利用物理学方法研究生物系统，生理学研究生物体功能），[1]但同时，他还研究南太平洋新几内亚岛的鸟类学*（研究鸟类）和生态学*（研究物种与环境的关系）。

1968年，戴蒙德被聘为加利福尼亚大学洛杉矶分校医学院的生理学教授。然而，是他的跨学科*研究方法（对不同学科的利用）奠定了其事业成功的基础。通过研究鸟类学，戴蒙德认识到对比相似环境下不同种群的方法颇具价值，后来他将这一方法运用于自己感兴趣的第三个研究领域——环境史学 *。环境史学与比较研究法 *（该方法体系需要分析两个或多个案例，以找出能解释各案例结果的相似点和不同点）的结合逐渐成为戴蒙德的标志，而他平易近人、讲故事般的写作风格进一步普及了这一方法。

这两种研究方法的结合大获成功。先前，戴蒙德尽管发表了诸多著作，但仅限于生理学、生态学和鸟类学领域。[2] 而在 20 世纪 90 年代，他所著的大众读物出版，他本人也随之愈加出名。继《第三种猩猩》（1991）获奖后，戴蒙德的另一部著作《枪炮、病菌与钢铁》（1997）也获得了普利策非虚构类奖等数个奖项。《大崩溃》（2005）是他的第四部著作。

《大崩溃：社会如何选择兴亡》的主要内容

戴蒙德在《大崩溃》中提出一个问题：史上一些文明在最终崩溃前，为何人口急剧减少，且政治、经济及社会复杂程度也大幅降低？他的答案是：这些文明的崩溃归咎于以下五个要素中的一个或多个：环境退化 *（生态系统因资源逐渐枯竭而衰退），包括人口过剩；气候变化 *；与敌为邻；贸易伙伴弱化；以及社会缺乏应对各类问题所需的文化资源。戴蒙德得出上述基本结论的方法是比较一系列历史文明，包括中美洲前哥伦布时期的玛雅文明 *（具体位于今墨西哥东南部、危地马拉、伯利兹、萨尔瓦多西部和洪都拉斯），格陵兰岛的诺尔斯（中世纪斯堪的纳维亚）殖民地文明，亨德森岛、皮特凯恩群岛和复活节岛的波利尼西亚文明，以及美国西南部的阿纳萨齐 *文明（这些远古居民的领地包括当今犹他州南部、亚利桑那州北部、新墨西哥州西北部及科罗拉多州西南部）。

这五个要素根据其数量及相互影响，以不同的方式结合。例如，对于诺尔斯殖民地文明不可阻挡的衰落，五个要素都发挥了作用。其中四个要素导致玛雅文明毁灭（除了贸易伙伴要素）。而阿纳萨齐文明瓦解的背后只有三个要素——森林砍伐 *（砍伐树木）、长期干旱，以及未能解决随之而来的社会问题。

戴蒙德指出，这些要素也可能损害当代全球社会，甚至带来毁灭。例如，五个要素中的一个或多个导致了近年来非洲国家索马里、卢旺达 * 和前南斯拉夫的衰落，而如今正在威胁伊拉克和印度尼西亚等国家。就连澳大利亚和美国都面临着风险，尤其是环境破坏问题，它可能是世界各国社会均面临的最大威胁。

仅一个要素便能触发急剧衰落的崩溃形势。太平洋东南部的复活节岛便是如此，在那里，人类大规模砍伐森林的行为无意中触发了连锁反应，导致生态的破坏与文明的毁灭。与之类似，全球工业强国所造成的污染可能会带来无法承受的损害。

因此，《大崩溃》敦促广大读者意识到人类活动在塑造人类文明未来中的重要作用，并采取补救措施，应对即将发生的环境灾难。

为寻找可能帮助我们解决问题的实践经验，戴蒙德再次审视过去的文明。他分析了几个案例，包括日本德川幕府时期 *（1603—1868）、太平洋蒂科皮亚岛和新几内亚高地，进而推断出可以结合以下方式避免生态灾难：克制、增长知识及价值论 * 灵活度，即社会改变其文化价值的能力。

相反，有些社会即使意识到了衰退，也"选择"不保证长期的可持续性 *。例如，诺尔斯人明知其邻居因纽特人更善于应对气候变化和其他颇具挑战的因素，然而其对宗教的盲目虔诚、强大的社会凝聚力以及对因纽特人的蔑视（认为因纽特人低人一等）使其不愿改变自身的文化价值，也不愿向邻居学习。戴蒙德总结道，类似的价值论僵化也阻碍了当今全球社会的选择，不利于推动**我们的**长期可持续发展。

《大崩溃：社会如何选择兴亡》的学术价值

戴蒙德在《大崩溃》中的结论关乎如今最具争议的话题之一：人类活动所引发的气候变化、其后果，以及我们的应对方法。事实上，他认为撰写这本书正是一个契机，可以向过去的社会学习如何应对环境问题。

我们关注这些问题，不仅因为意识到灾难即将到来，更因为人类对其所引发的气候变化的程度及后果缺乏共识。《大崩溃》一书表明，此种不确定性和随之而来的政治瘫痪——保守主义*——并不新奇。在过去，有些社会尽管意识到了衰落，却未必会采取措施挽回局势。

其实，戴蒙德认为社会崩溃与否在很大程度上取决于其文化价值以及政治、经济和社会制度。他提供了事实依据，证明人类活动的确改变了远古社会的发展进程，旨在说服我们，补救措施对于前人和今人而言同等重要。

不出所料，《大崩溃》一经出版便大受欢迎，已被译成31种语言。该书的成功不仅清楚表明戴蒙德所述的主题本身就颇具吸引力、受众广泛，也体现出作者身为大众作家的才华，能令大众了解复杂的历史问题及其与当今工业社会的关联。

读者不仅欣赏戴蒙德著作的内容，也喜欢其论证风格。他的另一部著作《枪炮、病菌与钢铁》基于所谓的"自然实验*（所研究情境受到的影响超出调查者的控制范围，调查者试图通过研究证明某种因果关系），比较了不同时空社会的异同，同样热销。另一方面，世界各地的专家学者——尤其是人类学家*（研究人类的学者）、考古学家*（研究远古人类活动的学者）、地理学家和历史学家——对此类"通俗"方法持批评态度。

然而，随之而来的争议也表明，这本书对于讨论如何学习过去社会的经验十分重要。尽管有些专家坚持认为，过去与现在之间有不可简化的差异，戴蒙德却提供了证据，说明两者之间也有诸多共同点。正是这些共同点塑造了人类，因此它们仍具参考价值和重要性。

---

1. 贾雷德·M.戴蒙德："胆囊浓缩活动"，博士论文，剑桥大学，1961 年。
2. 可参见贾雷德·M.戴蒙德等："新几内亚鸟类的食土癖"，《鹟》第 141 卷，1999 年第 2 期，第 181—193 页。

第一部分：学术渊源

1 作者生平与历史背景

要点 🔑

- 与之前的著作相同，戴蒙德在《大崩溃》中借鉴了数门学科的研究目的与方法，以回答关乎全人类的问题：社会缘何崩溃。

- 尽管戴蒙德受到专家的诸多批评，但他独到地融合了广泛的兴趣、多样的方法及平易近人的写作风格，使其著作享誉全球。

- 戴蒙德独特的研究风格源于其在生理学（研究生物系统功能）和鸟类学（研究鸟类）领域的工作、对人类学（研究人类）和环境的个人兴趣，以及田野考察和科学写作方面的经历。

为何要读这部著作？

贾雷德·M.戴蒙德在其畅销书《大崩溃：社会如何选择兴亡》（2005）中发问：为何有些社会崩溃瓦解，有些则没有？这是典型的"戴蒙德式"问题，类似于他在其普利策获奖著作《枪炮、病菌与钢铁》（1997）中所问的：为何有些社会占据主导地位，而有些却只能被主导？戴蒙德在《大崩溃》中回答问题的方式也体现了其典型的论证风格：全面比较不同时空社会的异同，以之为"自然实验"加以观察（例如，观察特定区域内的一群人，这群人会受到研究者控制范围之外的因素影响，目的是找出这些影响与观察到的变化之间的因果关系）。戴蒙德还解释了《大崩溃》的吸引力与他上一本书之间的关系："许多人……都在关注我的下一部作品，但另一个原因是这本《大崩溃》的主题确实吸引人。"[1]

"《大崩溃》的主题"是社会崩溃，其定义为"长期、大范围的人口急剧减少和／或政治／经济／社会复杂程度的大幅降低"。戴蒙德在《大崩溃》出版前便已探讨过这一主题。[2] 在书中，他指出五大要素的不同组合导致了过去及当今社会的崩溃。

戴蒙德的学术风格出自其对毕生所学的各门学科的融合。他的职业生涯始于生理学，并对鸟类学产生兴趣，而后研究历史，最终研究人种志[*]（研究不同人种及其风俗、习惯和信仰）。他的研究方法大获成功，所著的大众读物使他广受赞誉，包括《第三种黑猩猩》（1991）[3]、《枪炮、病菌与钢铁》（1997）[4]、《昨日之前的世界》（2012）[5] 及《性趣探秘》（1997）[6]。戴蒙德的学术旅程从自然与物理科学至社会科学和科普写作，而《大崩溃》是其中的又一座里程碑。

> "自从 20 多岁时读了托尔·海尔达尔关于复活节岛的书，我就对大型社会的崩溃产生了浓厚的兴趣——就像其他数百万人一样。过去 40 年来，这个兴趣始终没有消退，我参观了玛雅遗迹和阿纳萨齐遗址，阅读了社会崩溃方面的内容，兴趣更被激发。我起初并未将《枪炮、病菌与钢铁》和《大崩溃》规划为姊妹篇，可是……当我开始思考下一部书的主题时，答案就很清晰：大崩溃！"
>
> —— 企鹅阅读指南，"对话贾雷德·戴蒙德"

作者生平

贾雷德·M. 戴蒙德 1937 年出生于马萨诸塞州波士顿，双亲有东欧犹太人血统。戴蒙德与母亲一样，学习钢琴并萌发了对教学的兴趣。其父亲是儿科医师（专攻儿童医学），大概受父亲影响，戴蒙德取得了剑桥大学胆囊膜生理学博士学位。

同时，戴蒙德开始对鸟类学和生态学（研究物种与环境的关系）产生兴趣。他研究了太平洋新几内亚岛的鸟类和环境，并开始发表研究成果。关于这段经历，他说："幸好我那些有关鸟类的（学术）论文都发表在胆囊生理学家绝不会翻阅的期刊上……在学术界，研究多个领域并非有利，而是不利。"[7]

戴蒙德的第三个兴趣领域是环境史学（研究人类社会与环境的关系）。他也开始针对大众写作。在第二本书《枪炮、病菌与钢铁》问世后，戴蒙德便享誉全球，获得了诸多奖项。然而，这本书也招致了激烈的批评。由于书中的结论，学术界称他为文化帝国主义者 *（将自身文化价值观强加于他人）、环境决定论者 *（相信环境是社会结果的决定因素）以及激进经验主义者 *（拒绝考虑无法通过观察证实的证据）。

在《大崩溃》中，戴蒙德严肃地直面批评。他没有摒弃自然实验的激进经验主义和比较研究法（分析不同案例，以找出可能用于解释不同结果的异同点），还运用了人类学的人种志研究方法，丰富了研究的"工具包"。尽管受到同事和批评者的抨击，他毕生致力于融合各学科方法，力图回答关于人类的一般性问题。

创作背景

戴蒙德的背景深刻影响了其学术产出。攻读生理学博士使他确信，利用实验法分离变量的做法颇有价值。后来他利用此法研究相对孤立的社会的历史，如太平洋的蒂科皮亚岛和复活节岛上的社会。之后，戴蒙德在新几内亚研究鸟类学，需要比较鸟类的栖息地，以了解一组自变量 *（该术语来自数学，用于指代现象的外因）的影响。写作时，戴蒙德同样运用比较法，以了解人类社会的演变与一组自变量——如气候 *、生物多样性 *、动物群、大陆轴线 *——之间的关系。

实验与比较研究法的交汇，以及戴蒙德之后对环境史学和科普的兴趣孕育了他的著作《枪炮、病菌与钢铁》。这本书广受赞誉，但也令戴蒙德成为众矢之的，尤其受到人类学家的批评。在《大崩溃》中，戴蒙德直面批评，以人种志为第一章的内容。

这一章在很大程度上源于戴蒙德本人对美国西部蒙大拿州的认知。20 世纪 50 年代，十几岁的戴蒙德每年夏季都会在蒙大拿州待上几周。当时，他父亲诊治了一位农场主的儿子，两家因此结下了深厚情谊。[8] 此后，戴蒙德还在蒙大拿州购置了一处房产，更有机会洞悉蒙大拿人对本地命运的看法。

在这一章里，戴蒙德以知情者的视角，比较了有关水、空气和土壤污染的几个案例研究，以及其他影响蒙大拿州当今发展的主要问题。因此，他再次运用了人种志、自然实验和比较研究法。总之，《大崩溃》不仅比较了不同的社会，还融合了戴蒙德一生不断完善的方法论。

---

1. 企鹅阅读指南，"对话贾雷德·戴蒙德"，企鹅网站，日期未注明，登录日期 2015 年 9 月 9 日，www.penguin.com/read/book-clubs/collapse/9780143117001。
2. 贾雷德·M.戴蒙德："最后的印第安人：环境崩溃与文明终结"，《哈泼斯》杂志，2003 年 6 月；戴蒙德："复活节岛之终结"，《发现》杂志，1995 年 8 月；戴蒙德："失乐园"，《发现》杂志，1997 年 11 月。
3. 贾雷德·M.戴蒙德：《第三种黑猩猩：人类的身世与未来》，伦敦：哈珀柯林斯出版社，2006 年。

4. 贾雷德·M. 戴蒙德：《枪炮、病菌与钢铁》，伦敦：兰登书屋，2013 年。

5. 贾雷德·M. 戴蒙德：《昨日之前的世界：我们能从传统社会学到什么？》，纽约：维京出版社，2013 年。

6. 贾雷德·M. 戴蒙德：《性趣探秘：人类性的进化》，伦敦：阿歇特出版公司，2014 年。

7. 吉莉安·泰蒂："科学访谈：贾雷德·M. 戴蒙德"，《金融时报》，2013 年 10 月 11 日，登录日期 2015 年 9 月 30 日，www.ft.com/intl/cms/s/2/1f786618-307a-11e3-80a4-00144feab7de.html#axzz3jQUrhdub。

8. 贾雷德·M. 戴蒙德：《大崩溃：社会如何选择兴亡》，伦敦：企鹅出版集团，2011 年，第 27 页。

2 学术背景

要点 🔑

- 戴蒙德未必算是发现了新事物。其实，他的创新在于以新颖的方式分析并呈现已有材料。

- 人类社会与环境之间关系的研究始于"环境决定论"这一学派（该理论认为，某一区域内社会的历史轨迹由环境决定），戴蒙德与该学派关联密切。

- 撰写《大崩溃》一书时，戴蒙德在一定程度上受到前辈影响，利用过去崩溃社会的现有数据分析并拓展此前的社会崩溃理论。

著作语境

在贾雷德·M. 戴蒙德的《大崩溃：社会如何选择兴亡》出版之前，人类学家诺曼·约菲 *，人类学家兼考古学家乔治·考吉尔 *1、布莱恩·费根 *2，以及人类学家兼历史学家约瑟夫·泰恩特 *3 便已探索过社会崩溃这一主题。20 世纪 90 年代，研究人员愈发关注用环境影响解释社会崩溃的方法。例如，在自然科学领域各有所长的戴维·A. 霍德尔 *、贾森·H. 柯蒂斯 * 和马克·布伦纳 * 组成了研究团队，于 1995 年在《自然》杂志发表了一篇文章，提出气候变得更为干燥加速了前哥伦布时期玛雅文明的崩溃（该文明始于约 4 000 年前，分布在今天的墨西哥东南部，危地马拉、伯利兹、萨尔瓦多西部及洪都拉斯）。4 戴蒙德正是通过这些研究形成了综合研究方法，用于分析和吸取过去的经验教训。

环境史学家约翰·R. 麦克尼尔 * 解释说"环境史学家通常抵

触这样的主张"，即"总结过去的事件，为当今提供良药苦口的教训"。[5] 戴蒙德则恰恰相反，他建议视历史为科学，用以制定法律、预测未来，并指导当前事务。尽管无法在这些领域设置实验室条件 *（不像化学或物理），但仍可能开展所谓的"自然实验"，包括比较各种不受实验室条件限制的案例，其中存在或不存在潜在的关键变量。

例如，你可能注意到，复活节岛和玛雅文明崩溃时都经历了环境破坏，基于这一点便可假定环境破坏是崩溃的主要原因。然而，在推断崩溃与环境之间的关联时也要考虑差异。本例的关键是，复活节岛是太平洋中的一个孤立岛屿，而玛雅帝国却绝非孤立或边缘国度。这一差异突出表明，孤立状态并非崩溃的必要条件，而是一个可有可无的原因。

> "地理学家大都认为环境决定论是发霉过时的老古董。而多数地理学家并不大关注畅销书排行榜。"
>
> —— 詹姆斯·M. 布劳特："环境保护主义与欧洲中心论"

学科概览

20 世纪初，环境决定论在地理学领域盛行。这一理论可追溯至古希腊思想家，如哲学家柏拉图 *、亚里士多德 * 和医师希波克拉底 *，以及后来的哲学家，如活跃于 18 世纪的孟德斯鸠 *，他坚信环境因素导致了不同人口之间的种族、文化、社会及道德差异。环境决定论可概括为："寒冷的北方气候造就强健节俭之人"，而"赤道周围的持续酷暑则滋生懒惰之人"。[6]

20 世纪 20 年代，环境决定论受到美国地理学家卡尔·O. 索

尔 * 及其他所谓"文化可能论者" *7 的反对；他们认为，环境决定论将人类降格为环境的受体，因此无法解释人类对环境的改变。相反，他们提出了一种文化视角以理解人类与环境的关系。然而，这些观点运用起来颇为复杂，因为文化的定义有争议，一直以来都是争论不休的主题。起初，文化被视为文明的同义词，这一定义遭到批评，因其衡量并区分不同文化的文明程度。因此，出现了一种新趋势，即根据文化自身价值观、信仰和实践来定义各种文化。后来，为寻求统一的基本原则，学者开始研究每种文化的基本结构。文化被视为一种特定的话语，从中可以提取某种语法。但这种方法无法解释人类的主动性和变化。最终也未有某一定义被所有人一致接受。8

自 20 世纪 60 年代，文化就被视为人类与环境之间系统性相互作用的产物（即由人与环境所定义的系统内的相互作用）。9 之后，人类学家安德鲁·P. 韦达 * 和邦妮·J. 麦凯 * 提出关注个人行为，以明确系统内相互作用的具体路径。10 随后，又提出了更有章法的方式，将这些个人路径置于更广泛的政治和意识形态力量背景中。

《大崩溃》没有探讨这些不同的观点。戴蒙德并未论述人与环境关系方面的具体争论，而是以环境决定论的变体为立场参与讨论。戴蒙德没有将人类社会简单解释为不同环境作用下的产物，而是将环环相扣的多个因素归纳为理论，包括文化、政治，甚至偶然因素。

学术渊源

戴蒙德了解前辈学者为解释社会崩溃所做的尝试。例如，人类学家约瑟夫·泰恩特在《复杂社会的崩溃》（1988）中提出，当社会的复杂程度达到不可持续的境地时，它便会崩溃，因为社会无法产生足够的组织和物质能量，支撑其臃肿的*（过度生长、无法维持的）结构。[11]

泰恩特为得出这一结论，比较了三个崩溃案例：西罗马帝国、玛雅文明和美国西南部的阿纳萨齐文明，这一方法类似于戴蒙德的比较研究法。不过，泰恩特的结论是，所有社会都具备崩溃的特征，而戴蒙德基于更多案例样本指出有些社会可以避免此类危机。

戴蒙德也熟悉英国学者威廉·M. S. 拉塞尔*与克莱尔·拉塞尔*的论著《人口危机与人口周期》。两位学者同泰恩特一样，认为社会危机源于社会结构问题。[12] 两位学者认为，社会危机源于人口与支撑人口的资源增长幅度相异。社会要缓解人口增长压力，唯有采取控制生育之类的措施。该研究援引了中国、西非、西亚、地中海北部及欧洲西北部的例子。戴蒙德也提到，西南太平洋的蒂科皮亚岛民曾采用控制生育这一谨慎措施来避免社会崩溃。然而，他并不认为人口增长是社会崩溃的唯一或主要原因。确切地说，他认为社会崩溃有多种原因，而环境是一个主要原因。

这些研究在一定程度上影响了戴蒙德，为其提供了更多的案例研究。在理论方面，戴蒙德并未反对泰恩特的理论，即社会都有崩溃倾向，而是补充了这一观点，即社会若及时采取补救措施，便可渡过危机而幸存。同样，人口与支撑人口的资源之间增幅相异也会造成社会崩溃，这一理论正是戴蒙德在分析非洲卢旺达的崩溃时所采用的论述。

1. 诺曼·约菲和乔治·考吉尔编：《古老国家与文明的崩溃》，图森：亚利桑那大学出版社，1988 年。
2. 布莱恩·费根：《洪水、饥荒与君主：厄尔尼诺现象与文明的命运》，纽约：基础图书出版社，1999 年。
3. 约瑟夫·泰恩特：《复杂社会的崩溃》，剑桥：剑桥大学出版社，1988 年。
4. 戴维·A. 霍德尔等："气候在著名玛雅文明崩溃中可能发挥的作用"，《自然》第 375 卷，1995 年第 6530 期，第 391—394 页。
5. 约翰·R. 麦克尼尔："可用的过去"，《美国科学家》第 93 卷，2005 年第 2 期，第 172 页。
6. 戴维·科雷亚："去你的，贾雷德·戴蒙德"，《资本主义、自然、社会主义》第 24 卷，2013 年第 4 期，第 1—6 页。
7. 加布里埃尔·贾金斯等："人类与环境研究中的决定论及环境因果关系的重新发现"，《地理学期刊》第 174 卷，2008 年第 1 期，第 17—29 页。
8. 参见蒂姆·英戈尔德："文化概论"，载《人类学百科全书指南》，蒂姆·英戈尔德编，伦敦和纽约：劳特利奇出版社，1994 年，第 329—349 页。
9. 卡尔·W. 巴策："文化生态学"，载《美国地理》，加里·L. 盖尔与科特·J. 威尔莫特编，哥伦比亚：麦瑞尔出版社，1989 年，第 192—208 页；马文·哈里斯：《文化唯物主义：为文化科学而斗争》，纽约：兰登书屋，1979 年；罗伊·A. 拉帕波特，《献给祖先的猪：新几内亚人生态中的仪式》，纽黑文：耶鲁大学出版社，1968 年。
10. 安德鲁·P. 韦达和邦妮·J. 麦凯，"生态学与生态人类学的新方向"，《人类学年鉴》第 4 卷，1975 年，第 293—306 页。
11. 泰恩特：《复杂社会的崩溃》。
12. 克莱尔·拉塞尔与威廉·M. S. 拉塞尔："人口危机与人口周期"，《医学、冲突与生存》第 16 卷，2000 年第 4 期，第 383—410 页。

3 主导命题

要点 🔑

- 戴蒙德的著作《枪炮、病菌与钢铁》和《大崩溃》的核心是讨论人类社会命运以及研究人类社会历史的正确方式。

- 论战中的质疑者出于相似的原因批评戴蒙德的《大崩溃》及其之前的著作，原因包括环境决定论（认为社会发展及其结果仅由环境决定），以及将过去文明的崩溃归咎于文明自身。

- 如今的争论集中于批判环境决定论和西方帝国主义 *（一种意识形态，为欧洲强国统治非洲、大洋洲和美洲大片领土进行辩护）。批判者并非质疑《大崩溃》的整体结论，而是质疑戴蒙德的意识形态、方法论和理论方法。

核心问题

贾雷德·M. 戴蒙德的《大崩溃：社会如何选择兴亡》的核心是讨论所有社会崩溃的成因。通过比较一系列现代和古代社会的案例研究，戴蒙德指出，所有社会的崩溃都源于五个因素的组合。他提出，一些现代社会崩溃是因为它们无法解决过去社会也曾面临的同类问题。戴蒙德希望这一理论适用于过去、现在和未来的所有社会，并将得出这一综合理论的研究方法称为"比较环境史"*，这一方法与他在上一本著作《枪炮、病菌与钢铁》[1]中所采用的一样。由此可见，《大崩溃》不仅探讨了社会的失败，也体现出戴蒙德对其研究方法的信心。

《枪炮、病菌与钢铁》也因采用这一研究方法而受到批驳。批评者认为，将人类社会的命运仅仅归因于环境因素太过简单。他们认为，要想更全面地解释社会与历史的关系，还需要考虑权力关系和其他人类活动，而非只考虑所谓包罗万象的环境影响。

　　然而，戴蒙德在《枪炮、病菌与钢铁》中的论述并非如批评者所认为的那样简单。这一书名就列出了三个共同作用的成因。即使他用了相同的方法回答《大崩溃》所提出的问题（即多个因素的综合作用和环境的突出作用），也是因为他坚信该方法合理可靠。由此可见，《大崩溃》的核心不仅是对人类社会命运的思考，也是对戴蒙德研究方法的某种重申。

> "戴蒙德能获普利策奖，是因为他把这种荒唐的种族主义观点表达得如同常识一般。他的书不仅清洗了殖民暴力史，还为之杀菌消毒。"
>
> ——戴维·科雷亚："去你的，贾雷德·戴蒙德"

参与者

　　研究社会崩溃的理论家，如美国人类学家兼历史学家约瑟夫·泰恩特、英国学者威廉·M. S. 拉塞尔与克莱尔·拉塞尔，对《大崩溃》产生了主要的学术影响。戴蒙德并未反对或支持他们的理论，而是借鉴其思想和其他社会崩溃方面的研究，形成自己的理论。因此，围绕戴蒙德的争论焦点并非社会崩溃的根本原因，而是何种方法更适用于研究人类社会。

　　戴蒙德之前的著作的许多批评者也参与了这次争论。例如，有人类学家在"原始思维"网站上发文，质疑戴蒙德研究人类社会的方法是否可靠，尤其是该研究方法的伦理后果。人类学家的批判尤甚，因其认为戴蒙德的方法是决定论观点的基础，甚至体现了西方的优越感。[2]

批评者在《枪炮、病菌与钢铁》中看到了环境决定论的逻辑。该书认为，欧洲社会得以统治其他社会（尤其是美洲印第安人、澳大利亚原住民和非洲人），是因为 13 000 年前欧洲人在生物地理因素方面得天独厚，如气候较温和、有大陆轴线（大陆的水平假想线，该大陆领土的东西向距离长于南北向距离），以及有更多能够驯养的动物和培育的植物。原始思维网的博主认为戴蒙德的研究方法假定：若起点更好，任何社会都能发展农业、冶金等稳定社会所需的基础条件，早于自然条件较差的社会。因此，戴蒙德的方法被视为将影响人类社会的复杂命运简化为仅受环境影响。

而戴蒙德观点中的环境决定论假设可能引发的重大后果也受到质疑。批评者认为，主张环境是决定社会发展轨迹的根本原因，相当于间接认可欧洲的侵略、统治和殖民主义；换言之，欧洲人占据统治地位是因为享有得天独厚的环境条件；如果美洲印第安人、澳大利亚原住民或非洲人享有更好的环境，他们便会是统治者。

当代论战

戴蒙德并不信服这些批评，坚持认为环境和生态因素对人类历史和文化影响重大。同时，他并不否认文化和历史因素，甚至个人选择，都会影响人类社会的命运。戴蒙德认为，正确的研究方法介于以下两种极端之间：

- 基于详尽技术事实的地理和环境解释，
- 考虑历史和文化的作用。

在《大崩溃》中，当今辩论的影响清晰可见。在书中，戴蒙德直接探讨了决定论（认为每个事件都有预先确定的成因）[3]、简化论（将某一现象的成因归结为相对较少的因素，甚至单一因素）[4]，以及将社会命运归因于社会自身等问题。[5] 同时，他采用人类学家通常使用的人种志研究法，丰富自己研究的"工具包"，而人类学家正是戴蒙德最猛烈的抨击者。例如，第一章讲述蒙大拿州的生态问题，戴蒙德利用人种志补充其社会崩溃理论，并加入现今蒙大拿州人日常生活中的大量细节。

此外，他试图在寻找综合答案和对复杂情况的理解之间取得平衡。谈及这方面，他说："开始构思这本书时，我并未意识到这些复杂情况，还天真地以为这本书只关乎环境破坏……后来我意识到并没有纯粹的环境崩溃。"[6] 戴蒙德与批评者和解的结果便是《大崩溃》中的五点框架。该理论并非仅以环境因素解释所有社会命运的决定论观点，而是综合考虑了多个方面。然而，批评者并不一定对此感到满意。

1. 贾雷德·M. 戴蒙德：《枪炮、病菌与钢铁》，伦敦：兰登书屋，2013 年。

2. 克里姆·弗里德曼："从档案看：原始思维对决贾雷德·戴蒙德"，原始思维网，2012 年 1 月 22 日，登录日期 2015 年 9 月 30 日，http://savageminds.org/2012/01/22/from-the-archives-savage-minds-vs-jared-diamond/。

3. 贾雷德·M. 戴蒙德：《大崩溃：社会如何选择兴亡》，伦敦：企鹅出版集团，2011 年，第 20 页。

4. 戴蒙德：《大崩溃》，第 304 页。

5. 戴蒙德：《大崩溃》，第 324 页。

6. 阿莫斯·埃斯蒂："采访贾雷德·戴蒙德"，美国科学家在线网，日期未注明，登录日期 2015 年 9 月 30 日，www.americanscientist.org/bookshelf/pub/jared-diamond。

4 作者贡献

要点

- 尽管贾雷德·戴蒙德在《大崩溃》中基于证据，有条理地回答了一系列问题，然而答案是否令人满意取决于个人判断。

- 戴蒙德称自己的方法为"比较环境史"，即对比不同社会的深度案例研究，以提炼出能提供一般解释的关键变量。

- 《大崩溃》在理论、内容或方法上并无创新。其创新在于综合运用了数量空前庞大的社会崩溃案例研究。

作者目标

贾雷德·M.戴蒙德撰写《大崩溃：社会如何选择兴亡》一书有四个主要目标。第一，试图回答为何有些文明崩溃，有些则解决了自身面临的问题并繁荣发展。第二，试图找出不同文明崩溃的相似点。第三，讨论如何从存续及崩溃社会的命运中汲取经验教训，为当今提供借鉴。第四，也是最重要的一点，他表示，撰写《大崩溃》是为了提高民众对当今全球环境问题的意识，同时警醒人们，低估可能到来的崩溃会有何种风险。

戴蒙德开篇以人种志的方式描述蒙大拿州的环境问题，而后介绍了一系列案例研究，阐述他所选取的社会崩溃或存续的原因。他还对比了过去的社会与当代已崩溃或经历过危机管理的社会。基于对过去与现在、崩溃与存续社会的广泛对比，戴蒙德为当今社会总结出一系列实用的经验与教训。

尽管戴蒙德的论点有详尽的案例研究支持，但他援引的一些研究（如对美国西南部查科峡谷森林砍伐的研究）却因不尽准确而受质疑，这可能减损其观点的可靠性。此外，尽管《大崩溃》一书令环境保护主义辩论更受关注，也更具现实意义，但有人认为，戴蒙德对"坏"企业与意图保护环境的企业加以区分，反而有利于许多引发当今环境问题的大企业。[1]

> "因此，我 45 年的工作主业虽然不是地理或历史，它却意外地成了我如今在地理和历史领域事业的良好铺垫。"
> —— 贾雷德·戴蒙德："关于我"，www.jareddiamond.org

研究方法

戴蒙德称其研究方法为"比较环境史"，这一研究系统结合了生物学、地理学和历史学方法论，包括放射性碳定年法*（通过分析放射性标记物测定物体年代的方法）、考古学和植物学*调查，以及花粉和木炭分析*（通过分析植物残余测定某些植物在特定区域是否存在的方法），等等。例如，关于复活节岛崩溃原因的论述，其佐证包含花粉沉积物分析（提供了森林砍伐的证据），以及对垃圾堆中动物骨骼的研究（表明食物资源减少）。他还比较了这些分析与在其他地点开展的研究。

戴蒙德在《历史的自然实验》一书中概述了这一用于研究历史的多学科*比较法，该书由他与经济学家兼政治科学家詹姆斯·鲁滨逊*共同编写，包含 7 个案例研究。[2]该书解释说，尽管不可能将社会当作培养皿中的细菌来对待，但通过深入研究对比环境变量各异却情况相似的社会，也许能大体解释其命运。

例如，太平洋西南部的蒂科皮亚岛 3 000 多年来都能保持

1 200 左右的人口，这得益于资源微观管理和生育控制。同样，冰岛人由于学会了避免土壤退化，而成为全球人均收入 * 最高的群体之一。尽管这些社会相距甚远、各不相同，却有一个共同点：它们都学会了如何在不破坏环境的前提下获取资源。

关于比较研究法，戴蒙德写道："我已反复强调开展有效的个案研究和对比研究十分必要，因为学者若过多使用一种方法，就会轻视另一种方法的作用……对比研究结局不同的社会得到的证据才有分量，才可能得出令人信服的结论。"[3] 尽管在人类学领域这一研究方法不如使用已久、深入彻底的人种志法那般普遍，但也不算新鲜。

时代贡献

认定《大崩溃》一书仅对某一领域有所贡献并非易事。实际上，此书的贡献可见于人类学、考古学、历史学等诸多领域，因为这些领域的学者都质疑过《大崩溃》。戴蒙德没有直接谈讨此前有关文明崩溃的理论著作（如约瑟夫·泰恩特[4]、威廉·M. S.拉塞尔和克莱尔·拉塞尔等学者的著作），[5] 而是基于对这些案例研究的比较得出自己的论点。

在理论构建方面，《大崩溃》前所未有地综合了数量空前的社会崩溃案例研究。书中囊括了前人对崩溃社会的分析，以及此前社会崩溃方面的理论，并加以拓展，以涵盖崩溃因素所有可能的组合。如此，《大崩溃》贡献可观，如贡献于人类学家兼历史学家约瑟夫·泰恩特的结构崩溃论（该理论认为文化发展至不可持续的复杂程度时便会崩溃，因为无法产生足够的组织和物质能量支撑其过度发展的结构）。然而，戴蒙德的理论算不上彻底的突破，因其利用的几乎完全是已有的材料。

　　在内容方面，《大崩溃》并非基于一手数据，而是参考前人的深入研究。例如，关于诺尔斯（即现代之前的斯堪的纳维亚）殖民地崩溃的两章内容，与气候及岛屿考古学专家托马斯·麦戈文 * 的著作部分重合。[6] 又如，对比复活节岛与地球命运的做法先前已由考古学家保罗·巴恩 * 和古代尘埃颗粒分析专家约翰·弗伦利 * 共同提出。《大崩溃》中并无多少新内容，因此不被认为对社会崩溃研究有开创性的贡献。

　　在方法论方面，戴蒙德沿用了前人分析社会崩溃时的比较研究法。例如，约瑟夫·泰恩特比较了西罗马帝国、玛雅文明和北美阿纳萨齐文化的命运，指出社会复杂程度的降低导致这些社会的崩溃。[7] 戴蒙德认同这一研究方法，但加以拓展，以涵盖和综合大量案例研究。因此，他得出的结论与众不同，且影响更为深远。

---

1. 斯蒂芬妮·麦克米伦，"贾雷德·戴蒙德的买与卖"，counterpunch.org，2009 年 12 月 12 日，登录日期 2015 年 9 月 9 日，www.counterpunch.org/2009/12/08/the-buying-and-selling-of-jareddiamond/。

2. 贾雷德·M.戴蒙德和詹姆斯·A.鲁滨逊编：《历史的自然实验》，马萨诸塞州坎布里奇：哈佛大学出版社，2010 年。

3. 贾雷德·M.戴蒙德：《大崩溃：社会如何选择兴亡》，伦敦：企鹅出版集团，2011 年，第 17 页。

4. 约瑟夫·泰恩特：《复杂社会的崩溃》，剑桥：剑桥大学出版社，1988 年。

5. 克莱尔·拉塞尔和威廉·M. S. 拉塞尔:"人口危机与人口周期",《医学、冲突与生存》第 16 卷,2000 年第 4 期,第 383—410 页。

6. 托马斯·麦戈文等:"北部群岛、人为错误和环境退化:审视中世纪北大西洋的社会与生态变迁",《人类生态学》第 16 卷,1988 年。

7. 泰恩特:《复杂社会的崩溃》。

第二部分：学术思想

5 思想主脉

要点 🔑

- 贾雷德·M.戴蒙德指出，五个关键因素共同导致人类文明的崩溃，其中最重要的是第五个：社会应对其余四个因素的能力。
- 戴蒙德以过去社会的实例说明，为何有些社会受五个因素影响而瓦解消失，有些却能度过危机，幸免于难。
- 戴蒙德平衡了科学与通俗的文风，以讲故事的方式写就科学著作，既吸引读者，又传播知识。

核心主题

在《大崩溃：社会如何选择兴亡》一书中，贾雷德·M.戴蒙德指出有五大关键因素导致人类文明的崩溃。首先是环境退化，包括森林砍伐、污染、土壤退化、侵蚀*（雨、风、农业和森林砍伐导致土壤和岩石从一处移至另一处）和人口过剩。环境退化的程度取决于两个次要环境因素——脆弱度（易受损害的程度）和复原力*（恢复潜能）。这些次要因素反过来又取决于人类活动——如砍树、捕鱼的速度能否确保可持续发展，也取决于环境本身，环境或多或少能维持人类活动。

第二个因素是气候变化，这一因素曾经是自然存在的，如今却受人类活动影响，表现为降雨、温度和湿度等长期且大范围的变化。炎热、寒冷、潮湿、干燥，以及或多或少多变的气候导致干旱、难以忍受的极端气温、粮食减产和食物短缺。例如，玛雅地区曾遭受严重干旱，即如今墨西哥、危地马拉、伯利兹、萨尔瓦多西部、洪都拉斯和美国西南部的阿纳萨齐所在地区；同样，格陵兰岛上的诺尔斯（"维京"）殖民地没能熬过小冰期 *（气候史上的寒冷时期，1400 至 1800 年）。

第三个因素是近邻日益加剧的敌意。其实，"生态或其他原因所致的社会崩溃常常被掩饰为军事失利。"[1]

第四个因素与第三个相反，是友好邻邦支持与贸易的减少。的确，多数社会"都在一定程度上依赖友好邻邦……以进口必需的贸易商品。"[2]

第五个因素是社会应对自身问题的能力。对于一个社会的崩溃，前四个因素可能并非全都发挥重要作用，但第五个因素在各时各地都对社会的崩溃起重大作用。

因此，关键教训是，即使社会认识到了自身的问题，也不一定有能力解决。一个社会是否能够抵制上述某个因素或四个因素的联合作用，很大程度上取决于社会的文化价值观和政治、经济与社会制度。

> "有史以来，我们首次面临全球衰退的风险，但也首次享有契机，能迅速学习当今世界任何地方社会的发展，以及过去任何时期社会进程的经验。这是我撰写本书的原因。"
>
> —— 贾雷德·M. 戴蒙德：《大崩溃：社会如何选择兴亡》

思想探究

戴蒙德以过去社会的实例来说明为何有些社会受五个因素影响而瓦解消失，有些却得以存续。

太平洋东南部的复活节岛便是因第一个因素而崩溃的案例。其社会衰落是由于当地居民伐尽了岛上的棕榈树来制作独木舟和滚轮，以运送摩艾石像——零星环绕该岛屿的巨大石像。当地人不知道这种棕榈树不同于其他波利尼西亚群岛的棕榈树，无法迅速复原。此外，岛上各位酋长为扬名而竞争，将伐木活动推向了不归路。结果，岛上的动物逐渐灭绝，农业系统很快供给不足，无法养活全部人口，岛上居民最终走向内战及同类相食的境地。戴蒙德总结说，复活节岛"是最接近'纯粹'生态崩溃的案例，其具体原因是森林砍伐殆尽。"[3]

另一例是格陵兰岛的诺尔斯殖民地，其崩溃是五个因素共同作用的结果，尤其因为当地斯堪的纳维亚殖民者没能改变价值观并及时采取补救措施。对这些殖民者而言，"不可能仅仅为了在地球上多活一个冬季而减少对教堂的投资，模仿因纽特人的生活方式或与之通婚，并因此下地狱，永世不得超生。"[4]归根结底，是价值观僵化导致其社会崩溃。

反之，有三个社会克服了森林砍伐、侵蚀和土壤肥力丧失的问题，说明了灵活变通与及时补救的重要性。

17 世纪初，日本统治阶层德川幕府实行资源管理政策来解决森林砍伐问题，即便这意味着减少建造宏伟宫殿所需的木材供给。约 7 000 年前，巴布亚新几内亚高地人由于农业人口增长而出现木材危机，他们利用植物学知识（对于植物的研究）来提高土壤肥力并重新造林 *。

蒂科皮亚岛的酋长除了定期微观管理粮食生产外，还在公元 1600 年狠心屠宰了所有珍贵的猪，因其摧毁庄稼。戴蒙德写道，"即便猪是当时美拉尼西亚社会唯一的大型家畜，也是首要的社会地位象征"[5]，但岛民还是采取了这个措施。这些酋长与复活节岛的酋长不同，他们把生存看得比地位更重要。

语言表述

《大崩溃》与戴蒙德的其他著作一样，在文风方面的主要挑战是在科学与通俗语言之间找到适当的平衡。为了支持结论，戴蒙德在书中囊括了大量技术细节，涉及地理学、人类学、考古学和植物学等领域。他意识到，外行人甚至学生都可能缺乏必要知识，无法记住所有的技术细节，同时跟上文章的整体思路。因此，戴蒙德在陈述技术细节的同时讲述了一系列能做例证的轶事，以平衡文风。

例如，在阐释第五个因素时，戴蒙德写道，"复活节岛民在砍伐最后一棵棕榈树时说了什么？"[6] 为了说明资源管理的概念，他告诉我们，"正如我的挪威考古学家朋友克里斯蒂安·凯勒所言，'生活在格陵兰岛，关键要找到蕴含有用资源的好地方。'"[7] 此处，"马尔萨斯陷阱"* 理论十分重要，该理论由英国经济学家托马斯·马尔萨斯提出，指人口呈指数的增长往往会快于粮食产量的增长。谈及该理论时，戴蒙德探讨了卢旺达大屠杀（约有50至100万人丧生，大部分都是被胡图族人杀害的图西族人），他写道，"我的朋友1984年去卢旺达时便已感觉到生态灾难正在酝酿。"[8]

戴蒙德在书中常将远方国度的人称为"朋友"，这种表达有三个主要效果。首先，"为主题赋予具体的个人面孔，否则会显得抽象。"[9] 其次，将读者拉近话题，否则他们会感到陌生、遥远，甚至毫不相关。第三，将探索科学知识呈现得更像是世界"友人"间的对话，而非象牙塔中挑剔专家之间的艰苦辩论。

如此，戴蒙德创造出了一种讲解科学的叙述手法，既能吸引读者，又能传播知识。

---

1. 贾雷德·M.戴蒙德：《大崩溃：社会如何选择兴亡》，伦敦：企鹅出版集团，2011年，第11页。

2. 戴蒙德：《大崩溃》，第12页。

3. 戴蒙德：《大崩溃》，第18页。

4. 戴蒙德：《大崩溃》，第247页。

5. 戴蒙德：《大崩溃》，第521页。

6. 戴蒙德：《大崩溃》，第112页。

7. 戴蒙德：《大崩溃》，第210页。

8. 戴蒙德：《大崩溃》，第318页。

9. 戴蒙德：《大崩溃》，第30页。

6 思想支脉

要点 ⚷

- 虽然当今全球社会受到的威胁同样来自毁灭过往人类文明的五大因素，但当代社会能更好地应对这些挑战。

- 戴蒙德以当代及过往社会为例，说明古今社会面临相似的挑战，并总结如何规避崩溃危机的经验教训。

- 尽管过往社会遭受五大崩溃因素的严重打击，但有些社会并未完全消失。戴蒙德没有深入研究这种复原力，但探讨了为何有些社会得以存续。

其他思想

在《大崩溃：社会如何选择兴亡》一书中，贾雷德·M.戴蒙德先确定了导致社会衰败的主要因素，而后试图说明过去与现在的社会之间可找到相似之处。这些相似之处表明，社会若经历相同的过程，便会有相同的命运。如此，便可通过历史预测当代社会的崩溃。

过往和当今社会都有许多环境退化问题（戴蒙德论述的第一个因素）："过往社会破坏环境以致危及自身的过程可分为八类，其影响程度因案例而异，具体包括：森林砍伐与栖息地破坏、土壤问题（侵蚀、盐渍化*、土壤肥力丧失）、水资源管理*问题、过度捕猎、过度捕捞、引进物种对本地物种的影响、人口增长、可支配收入增加导致人类活动的影响增加。"[1]

此外，戴蒙德强调了一些重要的差异，鼓励我们考虑创新的解决方案，以避免当代社会的崩溃。"当今面临的环境问题除了危害过往社会的八个类别外，还有四类新问题：人为引起的气候变化、环境中有毒化学物质的增加、能源短缺，以及人类对地球光合能力 * 的完全利用。"[2] 全球化 *，即各大洲之间政治、经济和社会关系的日益趋同，导致了这四类新问题出现。

然而，全球化也有助于解决问题。"我们同样也首次享有契机，能迅速学习当今世界任何地方社会的发展，并汲取过去任何时期社会进程的经验。"[3] 戴蒙德以此暗示，撰写本书的行为便是例证，说明人类有能力反思过去，这是现代人与复活节岛民等过去居民的区别。

> "但是，现代世界及其问题与过去世界及其问题之间也有差异。不应天真地认为研究过去便能得出简单的解决方案，可直接挪用于当今社会。"
>
> —— 贾雷德·M. 戴蒙德：《大崩溃：社会如何选择兴亡》

思想探究

戴蒙德认为，过往社会与当代社会面临的问题都可大致划分为相同的类别，即五大关键因素。

例如，诺尔斯人（"维京人"）用尽了不可替代的草皮资源来造房屋、作燃料，这一点是其社会崩溃的重要原因。与之类似，美国、中国等当代社会正以不可持续的速度消耗燃料。燃料耗尽很可能（至少在一定程度上）致使无法找到可替代能源的社会面临崩溃。

又如，复活节岛民为提升酋邦 * 地位，以森林为代价建造大型雕像。同样，尽管地球资源有限，当今工业化社会似乎无法停止提高生产率。复活节岛民无法依赖贸易伙伴，地球居民同样也无法寻求其他星球的支持。因此，比起生产，我们更应珍视资源。

我们可以回顾历史，寻找方法解决当代社会面临的问题。日本德川幕府时期（1603—1868）避免了会引起自我毁灭的森林砍伐，得益于其风险意识，以及采取措施管理森林的意愿。同样，由于拉斐尔·特鲁希略*和华金·巴拉格尔*两位独裁者实施环境保护政策，多米尼加共和国避免了其邻国海地在 19 至 20 世纪经历的环境退化。

当今能否避免社会崩溃，很大程度上取决于我们能否应对戴蒙德所提出的 12 个环境问题。此外，戴蒙德指出，希望与绝望的迹象并存。他说，一些现代企业"对当下环境的破坏力最强，而有些则为环境提供了最有效的保护"。[4] 与过去一样，这些实力强大的商业竞争者可能选择牺牲社会利益以实现自己的目标，或者选择以可持续的速度发展。

被忽视之处

《大崩溃》中被忽视的方面是戴蒙德承认崩溃与存续往往共存。书中，戴蒙德在整体上更侧重论述社会崩溃，而非社会残余或幸存之人。这也许并不令人意外，也颇为合理，毕竟这本书主要关乎崩溃，而非存续或复原力。然而，戴蒙德确实承认，有些人在社会崩溃中幸存。例如，他指出，灭绝的北美阿纳萨齐人并未完全消失，在当代美洲原住民社会中便有其后代。[5]

戴蒙德认识到崩溃社会有一定的复原力，但这一点并未得到多少学术认可。比如，人类学家帕特里夏·麦卡纳尼*和诺曼·约菲认为戴蒙德没有认识到任何社会都不会简单消失，这一点大大削弱了戴蒙德论点的说服力。[6]戴蒙德确实只简要提及阿纳萨齐及其他崩溃社会的后代，并未进一步分析其存续，但重要的是他至少提到了存续现象，通过补充描写持久力与适应力的情形，平衡了"崩溃是人口极度缩减与文化丧失"的观点。

麦卡纳尼和约菲批评戴蒙德低估了社会的复原力。例如，他们反对戴蒙德关于玛雅帝国崩溃的论点，指出尽管8至9世纪一些玛雅城市人口急剧减少，但同期玛雅帝国其他地区的人口却增加了。此外，玛雅后裔在玛雅文明后古典时期*（约950—1539年）依然活跃在人口稠密的城市，目前也有700万人居住在墨西哥和中美洲北部。

若充分结合崩溃与复原这两个概念，便可能在理论方面更深刻地解读人类社会。例如，可以认为崩溃是破坏性创造的过程，社会在此过程中发展新文化，从而重新定义自身与环境的关系。

---

1. 贾雷德·M.戴蒙德：《大崩溃：社会如何选择兴亡》，伦敦：企鹅出版集团，2011年，第4页。

2. 戴蒙德：《大崩溃》，第5页。

3. 戴蒙德：《大崩溃》，第11页。

4. 戴蒙德：《大崩溃》，第11页。

5. 戴蒙德：《大崩溃》，第135页。

6. 帕特里夏·A.麦卡纳尼和诺曼·约菲编：《质疑崩溃：人类复原力、生态脆弱性与帝国的未来》，纽约：剑桥大学出版社，2010年。

7 历史成就

要点 🔑

- 尽管戴蒙德在《大崩溃》中提出的观点未必有所突破，但该书仍然有许多优点，使其颇受赞誉。
- 《大崩溃》最重要的成就是提供基于证据的论述，以支持虽有争议但传播广泛的观点：拯救地球有赖于治理环境。
- 《大崩溃》虽然是畅销书，却不及戴蒙德此前的著作《枪炮、病菌与钢铁》成功，也许因为他试图融入太多内容，导致该书篇幅更长，可读性更弱。

观点评价

贾雷德·M.戴蒙德在《大崩溃：社会如何选择兴亡》一书中完成了自己的预定目标。他比较研究了大量过去与当今社会的案例，以此建立社会崩溃的一般理论，并总结出导致社会崩溃的五大关键因素。然而，尽管他的观点论据翔实、论述清晰，却并未突破此前社会崩溃方面的认知。

戴蒙德列出了导致崩溃的五大关键因素，但只是重组和验证了先前的结论，并基于更广泛的案例对比加以拓展。同样明显的是，崩溃的关键因素，即社会采取补救措施的能力，即便对环境问题的相关辩论有可观的影响，但对社会崩溃的作用或许不言自明。[1]

由此可见，戴蒙德十分强调环境是社会崩溃的主要原因（但也承认其他因素的作用，如与邻近群体的关系）。然而，他还认为，社会应对自身衰落的能力首先取决于其价值观，换言之，取决于文化。戴蒙德坚持认为文化是可能从崩溃中拯救社会的最重要因素。因此，戴蒙德似乎认为环境与文化同等重要。

> "如果我有能力和手段改变当今世界上的一件事，那我会选择改变'我只能改变一件事'的局限：我想赋予自己能力去改变更多。原因就如我在《大崩溃》最后一章中所讨论的一样，我们面临 12 个不同的大问题，所有问题都必须成功解决，否则即便解决了 11 个，最后那个也会置我们于死地。"
>
> —— 企鹅阅读指南，"对话贾雷德·戴蒙德"

当代成就

戴蒙德写《大崩溃》时并未使用太多一手（"原始"）研究资料，大多采用个人经历，只为给读者讲述轻松轶事，令分析更加浅显易懂。他的基本观点主要依据前人在历史、人类学、考古学和环境领域的研究，从中提炼精华，形成自成一体的答案。

如此，不可否认，戴蒙德对社会崩溃研究的贡献重大。他的研究着实表明，从众多各异的研究中捋清交织的线索绝非易事。

戴蒙德著作的成功还可见于当前对环境问题讨论的重视，以及书中结论带来的政治影响。戴蒙德认为，影响社会崩溃的一个关键因素是社会，尤其是社会领袖扭转颓势的能力。正如历史上太平洋蒂科皮亚岛、日本德川幕府时期（1603—1868）及现今的多米尼加共和国之例，其领袖可通过施行某些政策改变社会命运。

《大崩溃》的广泛成功也归功于戴蒙德的第二本书《枪炮、病菌与钢铁》[2]，该书获得多个奖项，翻译为 25 种语言，销量超过 100 万册。喜爱书中大量文化比较的读者期待再读一本综合世界社会盛衰案例的鸿篇巨制，即便不认同该书的人也同样期待。

然而，与《枪炮、病菌与钢铁》一样，相较专家群体，《大崩溃》更受普通大众欢迎。专家认为这本书缺陷诸多、充满偏见，且在许多方面有明显错误。相反，公众并不一定关注该书背后的意识形态或学界认为的不尽精准之处。非专业人士看重的是案例论述清晰充分，得出的结论支持了已然广泛传播的观点：若想拯救地球，必须明智地治理环境。这或许是《大崩溃》最重要的成就。

局限性

戴蒙德认为第五个因素——社会采取补救措施以避免崩溃的能力——是社会生存最重要的因素，这也是唯一一个所有崩溃案例分析中他都提到的因素。尽管如此，戴蒙德并未真正解释这一因素所包含的内容。

戴蒙德显然认为，15 世纪格陵兰岛诺尔斯社会之所以崩溃，是因为诺尔斯殖民者无法改变价值观，向当地因纽特人学习如何更好地适应环境。同样，复活节岛居民似乎理应在 15 至 17 世纪间发起文化变革，如此便不会为了运送雕像和制作独木舟而砍伐整片森林。然而，戴蒙德并未解释改变文化究竟意味着什么。

戴蒙德在描述社会避免崩溃的案例时则有力得多，比如日本幕府实施树木管理政策，以及巴布亚新几内亚高地自下而上对园艺加以微观管理。换言之，不难想象推行这些单独的决策是为了更高层面的裨益。但该书没有解释清楚的是，这些单独的决定如何能被视作民族文化的表达，而非当时情形催生的应对决策。

戴蒙德的研究大部分基于大范围对比，因此或许能从中剥离出文化的一种定义：能随情况变化而调整的一套价值体系。即便算不上明确提出，戴蒙德也确实根据其跨文化的比较暗示过这一概念。不过，尽管文化是戴蒙德理论的核心，在《大崩溃》中，它的定义却并不透彻。

1. 威廉·里斯："沉思深渊"，《自然》第 433 卷，2005 年第 7021 期，第 15—16 页。
2. 唐纳德·肯尼迪："选择：在环境破坏的历史中寻找希望"，《外交》第 84 卷，2005 年第 2 期，第 134 页。

8 著作地位

要点 ☠

- 继《枪炮、病菌与钢铁》名声大噪后，戴蒙德的《大崩溃》一书出版。不出所料，两本书在风格、研究方法和主要研究问题方面都有许多共同之处。

- 《大崩溃》融合了戴蒙德生活中的许多方面，包括其职业生涯、个人经历，以及他与公众、同事、朋友，甚至敌人之间的关系。

- 《大崩溃》虽不是戴蒙德最成功的著作，但展现了戴蒙德的学者生涯：始于硬科学*，而后转向社会科学和科普写作。

定位

《大崩溃：社会如何选择兴亡》于 2005 年出版，那时贾雷德·M. 戴蒙德已是世界知名学者。他的著作《第三种黑猩猩》[1] 令其走入公众视野，该书荣获 1992 年罗恩—普朗科学书籍奖和《洛杉矶时报》图书奖。

戴蒙德的第二本书《枪炮、病菌与钢铁》[2] 享誉世界，获得多个奖项，包括 1998 年的普利策奖、安万特科学书籍奖和 1997 年美国大学优等生协会科学奖。戴蒙德的职业生涯于 1997 年达到高峰，另一畅销著作《性趣探秘》在同年出版。

之后，戴蒙德花了 5 年多时间研究和分析用于撰写《大崩溃》的素材。他已十分擅长整合大量用于对比的材料，涉及全球各地，时间跨度长达 13 000 年。

戴蒙德在《枪炮、病菌与钢铁》一书中使用比较研究法提出并解答为何欧洲人能征服澳大利亚、非洲和美洲的土著居民，而非反之。他的答案是诸多环境原因以及随之而来的一系列反馈环（持续自我改善的循环）。戴蒙德在《大崩溃》中使用相同的比较研究法，回答了另一个可能相关的问题：社会缘何崩溃？他的答案依然是诸多环境因素，这些因素使一些社会发展相对顺利，另一些则较为坎坷。

尽管戴蒙德并没有视《大崩溃》为《枪炮、病菌与钢铁》的姊妹篇，但二者之间明显有知识联系。

> "戴蒙德虽不是人类学家，但他大概是人类学领域最知名的作家！"
> —— 帕特里夏·A. 麦卡纳尼和诺曼·约菲：《质疑崩溃》

整合

戴蒙德的学术生涯对其著作有不可否认的影响。他早年攻读生理学博士学位期间，开始发表胆囊研究方面的专业文章。后来，他尝试分享自己在生理学方面的兴趣，大胆撰写了面向大众读者的《第三种黑猩猩》。

同时，戴蒙德对鸟类学也颇有兴趣，日益频繁地比较不同的鸟类种群。20 世纪 90 年代，在撰写《枪炮、病菌与钢铁》的过程中，他结合了自己的科普写作能力、对比较研究法的兴趣，以及对人类历史新近萌发的着迷。这部著作成就了戴蒙德，使其成为近十年来最重要的科学家之一。

然而，学术界对《枪炮、病菌与钢铁》并非一致认可。戴蒙德十分重视学术批评，《大崩溃》明显体现了他力图避免民族中心主义*（倾向于采用本族文化理论和价值观审视及评价他人的文化）、社会达尔文主义*（声名狼藉的概念，认为个人及社会都如生物物种，受制于相同的进化压力）和环境决定论（某一区域的环境决定其中社会的历史路径）等方面的言论，以避免相关指责。

例如，他赞扬日本德川时期的幕府、蒂科皮亚岛的波利尼西亚人和巴布亚新几内亚高地人，认为这些非西方社会管理环境资源有方。这么做似乎是为了避免民族中心主义方面的指责。又如，《大崩溃》第一章更像是人种志（研究某一民族的风俗、习惯和信仰），而非广泛比较。

因此，与《枪炮、病菌与钢铁》相比，《大崩溃》包含更多人种志、技术篇章及具体学术辩论。而且相比《枪炮、病菌与钢铁》，戴蒙德在《大崩溃》中更频繁地暗示自己的反种族主义立场，仿佛重复可以澄清他认为自己早已说明的观点。这些似乎都是为了避免评论人士的抨击。

意义

尽管《大崩溃》并非戴蒙德最成功的著作，但该书展现了他的学者生涯，他起步于所谓的硬科学，而后转向社会科学，解决他认为关乎人类的关键问题。为此，他采用了自称为"比较环境史"的方法（用于形容一种研究人类社会的方法，即深入比较案例以找出关键变量，从而得出一般性解释）。戴蒙德还采用平易近人的语言，尽量拓宽受众面。

虽然戴蒙德因此受到公众的赞誉，但也遭到专家的广泛抨击。这使他在运用智慧才能的同时，也对理论抱有谦逊之心。[3] 他继而以彻底批判的方式向社会科学家展示了"比较环境史"的作用。

争议双方似乎都有所收获，但这并不意味着戴蒙德与批评他的学术人士之间的争论已然罢休。戴蒙德常被指责是早期西方帝国主义的捍卫者和地理决定论 * 的拥护者。

矛盾的是，戴蒙德在《大崩溃》和《枪炮、病菌与钢铁》中都表明，文明成败并不取决于种族优势。相反，戴蒙德认为社会的发展和崩溃或多或少归因于环境，同时，崩溃和复原也受机缘等其他因素影响。这表明戴蒙德的理论推崇多发性原因 *（简言之是指一个事实由多种原因造成），而非评论人士所说的决定论。如此，无论对他的批评是什么，这两本书都是有力的案例。

戴蒙德著作的意义也在于他所传递的信息，即历史和科学不一定是专属于学术精英的专业领域。戴蒙德对自己如何构思《大崩溃》的解释，听起来仿佛任何人都写得出，只要有足够的兴趣并足够自律："这很简单。这是我能想到的最吸引人、最重要的主题，也是我几十年来一直感兴趣的主题，就像许多人对崩溃社会的遗迹有幻想和兴趣一样，比如丛林掩藏的玛雅遗迹或是美国沙漠中的阿纳萨齐高大建筑。这种浪漫的谜团吸引了我。"[4]

因此，《大崩溃》的一大价值是令公众意识到科学和历史也可以妙趣横生。该书平易近人，使读者可就一些十分引人入胜的人类问题形成自己的看法。

---

1. 贾雷德·M.戴蒙德：《第三种黑猩猩：人类的身世与未来》，伦敦：哈珀柯林斯出版社，2006 年。

2. 贾雷德·M.戴蒙德:《枪炮、病菌与钢铁》,伦敦:兰登书屋,2013年。

3. 可参见:约翰·R.麦克尼尔:"可用的过去",《美国科学家》第93卷,2005年第2期,第172—175页。

4. 阿莫斯·埃斯蒂:"贾雷德·戴蒙德访谈",《美国科学家》(网页版),日期未注明,登录日期2015年9月30日,www.americanscientist.org/bookshelf/pub/jared-diamond。

第三部分：学术影响

9 最初反响

要点 🔑

- 《大崩溃》受到好评，因其在环境问题辩论中提出了一个有力、浅显易懂且受众面广的观点。但该书的研究方法及所谓的意识形态前提遭到猛烈抨击。

- 尽管戴蒙德在《大崩溃》中已针对可能面临的批评撰写了"预防性的回应"，然而该书依然遭到批评。戴蒙德在相关期刊中发表了回应。

- 围绕《大崩溃》的争论颇为尖刻——这或许源于评论家眼中该书所蕴含的政治、意识形态和道德意味，而非由于该书的内容。

批评

贾雷德·M.戴蒙德的《大崩溃：社会如何选择兴亡》在美国一经出版，几天内便成为畅销书，这或许有赖于戴蒙德前作《枪炮、病菌与钢铁》的大获成功。[1]《大崩溃》在世界重要的报纸杂志上都广受好评。总体而言，正面评价《大崩溃》的人赞同戴蒙德提出的观点，并认可其对社会的实际影响。

例如，气候及可持续发展领域学者威廉·里斯*指出，当下有关环境问题的辩论总体尚无定论且缺乏共识，而《大崩溃》则提出了有力观点。[2]里斯赞扬戴蒙德在书中点明：纵观人类历史，影响社会环境命运的关键变量一直都是人类的责任，尤其领袖的责任。

戴蒙德受到称赞的原因还在于他能广泛吸引读者，这些读者学科背景各异，或先前不具备任何相关学科知识。[3]事实上，就连批评戴蒙德的人也承认，学术专业化"令感兴趣的外行和好奇的学生产生距离感。"[4]

然而，评论人士抨击《大崩溃》针对的是支撑观点的研究方法和所谓的意识形态出发点。这些负面评价可分为四个主题。

首先，评论人士认为《大崩溃》"仍坚持环境决定论的逻辑……美其名曰'新环境决定论'。"[5]换言之，评论家坚持认为，戴蒙德仅仅将人类社会的成败看作环境条件的产物。

第二，评论人士坚持认为戴蒙德的环境决定论是在维护西方帝国主义（笼统而言，这种意识形态将欧洲强国统治非洲、大洋洲和美洲大片领土的行为合理化）。人类学家弗雷德里克·K.埃林顿*恰当地总结了这一观点："富国因机缘巧合而繁荣，穷国则要为自己的消亡负责。"[6]

第三，戴蒙德未能认识到任何社会都不可能完全消失，这似乎会损害"崩溃"一词的有效性。例如，当今仍能找到玛雅人的后裔以及美国西南部的印第安人等。专门抨击戴蒙德著作的《质疑崩溃》尤其强调这一点。[7]

第四，评论人士指责戴蒙德忽视了某些事实。例如，考古学家兼人类学家特里·亨特*和考古学家卡尔·利波*认为复活节岛的森林砍伐由掠食性波利尼西亚鼠引起，而非岛民所致，因为岛上的人口数量一直保持稳定，直至欧洲人带来疾病和奴隶制，[8]人类学家本尼·派泽*也指出了这一点。[9]

> "威尔科克斯*认为，'查科峡谷的伟大建筑是社会败绩'这一观点算是一例'逆向工程'，即以过去的失败解释当代民众被剥夺经济和政治权利之苦，认为这是殖民扩张和欧洲后裔所带来的直接后果。"
>
> —— 帕特里夏·麦卡纳尼和诺曼·约菲：《质疑崩溃》

回应

从某种意义而言，戴蒙德无需回应关于环境决定论的指责，因为他已在《大崩溃》中表明，自己的观点并非简单的决定论，而是基于诸多因素。如一位学者所言："环境退化往往是众多力量中的一股。"[10] 然而，戴蒙德还是在很多场合回应了包括上述在内的许多批评。

戴蒙德坚持认为这些批评都带有偏见，暗含"所有地缘解释都是种族主义"的假设。他认为，批评者们仍在盲目针对 19 和 20 世纪社会科学中的种族主义倾向。[11]

关于文化帝国主义的指责，戴蒙德表示，他并不认为已经崩溃的社会是咎由自取，而意在赞扬那些采取补救措施的个人和群体。例如，多米尼加共和国制定的预防政策说明"如果领袖不只是被动地应对时局，而是有勇气预测危机、及早行动，并能做出富有远见的有力决策，进行自上而下的管理，便真能为社会带来巨大的变化"。[12]

关于崩溃的定义，戴蒙德认为，"若在一个社会中，所有人都难逃一死，或者大多数人口都将消亡，又或者几个世纪以来都没有文字作品、政府机构和伟大艺术，那便没有道理将其重新定义为'具有令人振奋的复原力'。"[13] 戴蒙德认为，只有那些对动植物、土壤和气候缺乏基本常识的人才会否认环境退化造成的破坏。[14]

根据历史史实，戴蒙德指出，复活节岛的森林砍伐与老鼠无关，这些老鼠也存在于波利尼西亚群岛的其他地方，但并未引起森林砍伐。他补充说，亨特和利波这些结论"显然错误，几乎所有现行在复活节岛开展研究的其他考古学家都如此认为。"[15]

冲突与共识

戴蒙德与其批评者之间能否达成一定的共识，很大程度上取决于争论基调和批评内容。例如，戴蒙德写道："每当听到'地理决定论'，我就知道又会是对地理因素的反射性驳斥，是不值一听、不值一读的观点，是思想偷懒的借口，并未抓住实质问题。"曾有记者问戴蒙德，是否有批评令他反思《大崩溃》的某些方面，他答道："细节方面，有；紧要观点方面，没有。"[16] 由此可见，有些批评者指出的不准确之处确有道理，有些则缺少证据、站不住脚。

但总体而言，戴蒙德与评论家之间的距离意味着双方不太可能达成一致。论点站不住脚，往往因为缺乏能力或专业知识。例如，戴蒙德若说评论人士不是专业的地理学家，[17] 这些人便回敬说戴蒙德不是专业的历史学家。[18] 此类争论并不总是有成效。

争论双方无法平等地讨论，并非由于戴蒙德在《大崩溃》中的论述所致，该书主要是对过往学者观点的整合。批评者们言辞尖刻，更多源于他们所认为的《大崩溃》所代表的政治观点、意识形态和道德立场——或许这才是他们真正反对的。

1. 唐纳德·肯尼迪："选择：在环境毁坏的历史中寻找希望"，《外交》第 84 卷，2005 年第 2 期，第 134—138 页。

2. 威廉·里斯："沉思深渊"，《自然》第 433 卷，2005 年 1 月 6 日第 7021 期，第 15—16 页。

3. 约翰·R. 麦克尼尔："可用的过去"，《美国科学家》第 93 卷，2005 年 3 月 1 日第 2 期，第 174 页。

4. 帕特里夏·A. 麦卡纳尼和诺曼·约菲编：《质疑崩溃：人类复原力、生态脆弱与帝国的未来》，纽约州纽约：剑桥大学出版社，2010 年，第 4 页。

5. 加布里埃尔·贾金斯等："人类与环境研究中的决定论与环境因果关系的重新发现"，《地理学杂志》第 174 卷，2008 年第 1 期，第 18 页。

6. 乔治·约翰逊："社会衰落，责任于谁"，《纽约时报》，2007 年 12 月 25 日，登录日期 2015 年 9 月 30 日，www.nytimes.com/2007/12/25/science/25diam.html。

7. 麦卡纳尼和约菲：《质疑崩溃》。

8. 特里·亨特和卡尔·利波："生态灾难、崩溃以及拉帕努伊（复活节岛）的生态灭绝之谜"，载《质疑崩溃》，麦卡纳尼和约菲编，第 223—246 页。

9. 本尼·派泽："从种族灭绝到生态灭绝：拉帕努伊的踱蹒"，《能源与环境》第 16 卷，2005 年第 3 期，第 513—540 页。

10. 麦克尼尔："可用的过去"，第 172 页。

11. 贾雷德·M. 戴蒙德："地理决定论：'地理决定论'究竟什么意思？"，jareddiamond.org，日期未注明，登录日期 2015 年 9 月 30 日，www.jareddiamond.org/Jared_Diamond/Geographic_determinism.html。

12. 贾雷德·M. 戴蒙德，《大崩溃：社会如何选择兴亡》，伦敦：企鹅出版集团，2011 年，第 304 页。

13. 贾雷德·M. 戴蒙德："崩溃的两个观点"，《自然》第 463 卷，2010 年第 7283 期，第 881 页。

14. 戴蒙德："地理决定论"。

15. 马克·莱纳斯："复活节岛之谜——贾雷德·戴蒙德的回应"，marklynas.org，2011 年 9 月 22 日，登录日期 2015 年 9 月 10 日，www.marklynas.org/2011/09/the-myths-of-easter-island-jared-diamond-responds/。

16. 企鹅阅读指南，"对话贾雷德·戴蒙德"，penguin.com，日期未注明，登录日期 2015 年 9 月 9 日，www.penguin.com/read/book-clubs/collapse/9780143117001。

17. 戴蒙德："地理决定论"。

18. 安东尼·J. 麦克迈克尔："大崩溃：社会如何选择兴亡。贾雷德·戴蒙德"，《国际流行病学杂志》第 35 卷，2006 年 4 月 1 日第 2 期，第 499—500 页。

10 后续争议

要点 ⚷

- 可以说，在关于土著权利和西方帝国主义的学术争论中，戴蒙德的观点被歪曲了。

- 戴蒙德与其反对者之间的大部分争论都聚焦于不同的知识研究方法，关于比较法的实用及可行程度。

- 目前在学术界，由于戴蒙德与许多人类学家之间不可调和的敌意，有关事实证据和研究方法的讨论停滞不前。

应用与问题

学界讨论是否采纳贾雷德·M.戴蒙德《大崩溃：社会如何选择兴亡》中的观点时，所遇到的问题是，关于该书价值的争议不一定源于书中观点，而是源于批评者所声称的书中观点。例如，在《去你的，贾雷德·戴蒙德》一文中，美国学者兼社会活动家戴维·科雷亚＊写道："戴蒙德的一切所为都由环境决定论驱动，该理论认为气候等物理环境是人类社会的决定因素。"[1] 然而，正如戴蒙德所解释的，"严格来说，如今任何明智的人都不会认同（环境决定论），但凡还敢探讨环境如何影响历史的历史学家常被批评者讽刺为'环境决定论者'，据说是指这些人相信人类历史完全由环境决定，而人类的选择毫无作用。"[2] 似乎《大崩溃》与《枪炮、病菌与钢铁》一样，都被视为环境决定论这一古老学派的产物，即便书中内容并不一定支持环境决定论的思想。

因此，决定论方面的指责并不一定关乎《大崩溃》中的观点。

争论之所以如此激烈，或许更多源于戴蒙德与批评者之间由来已久的紧张关系。例如，一些人类学家指责戴蒙德，认为其理论支持"帝国资本主义意识形态"——地理学家迪克·皮特*如是说[3]（资本主义是当今西方社会主导的社会经济制度，贸易和工业由私人掌控）。另一些人类学家则自视为土著权利的捍卫者，对抗他们眼中全球化（各大洲政治、经济、文化联系与习惯的融合）的同质化力量和西方资本主义引起的社会经济不平等。[4] 两种观点都不一定合理，因为戴蒙德从未明确地为西方帝国主义的正当性辩护，也没有哪个土著群体认为自己需要某些人类学家提出的那种保护。但可以说，在争论之中，戴蒙德曾因一些自己没提出过的观点而遭到抨击。

> "戴蒙德提出的框架超越了生态崩溃的简化构想，他认识到环境退化只是诸多力量中的一股，有时还会与其他力量协同作用。"
>
> ——约翰·R. 麦克尼尔："可用的过去"

思想流派

另一种解读关乎《大崩溃》在一般规律研究*与特殊规律研究*之争中的作用。一般规律研究尝试从特定事实中提取一般想法或法则；特殊规律研究则假定没有任何现象真正可比，只有具体属性才值得描述。

两种研究方法之争由来已久，而戴蒙德构思其著作时争议犹在。1988 年，曼彻斯特大学有过辩论，人类学家投票表决人类学是否属于归纳一般规律的科学，37 位人类学家反对，26 位赞同。

近 30 年后，人类学家亚历克斯·戈卢布＊写道，"（美国）人类学家希望向世界传播的唯一经验是'人类学很复杂'。无论在课堂还是出版物里，我们的目标都是向受众展现人类生活的复杂性。令一般规律研究或模式化学科愕然的是，'抽象'和'简化'对我们而言往往是贬义词。"5 由此可见，有关人类学的争议今日犹存。

戴蒙德创作《大崩溃》，不一定是要说服批评者，使其相信跨文化比较和自然实验是绝对可靠的科学方法。然而，人类学家对该书的质疑针对的是涉及人类社会各方面的一般观点，这些观点对立于强调人类学复杂性的观点，使人类学家感到不满。

对人类学复杂性的强调至少可追溯至先锋人类学家弗朗茨·博厄斯＊的时代，他认为不可能构建人类社会的一般理论。他坚持认为，人类学的目标是人种志的描述，依据是他所谓的"历史特殊论"（简言之，任何社会都是其独特历史环境的产物）。然而，其他人类学家仍然尝试构建一般理论。例如，在 1925 年，法国颇有影响力的社会学家马塞尔·莫斯＊基于跨文化比较研究撰写了《礼物》一书，该书大概是人类学领域最受欢迎的著作。

由此可见，一般规律研究与特殊规律研究之间的对立是人类学固有的争议，而非人类学家反对戴蒙德观点的原因。

当代研究

专家认为，戴蒙德的著作大获成功、广受欢迎，极不利于其观点的传播。的确，他的观点一再被盗用和歪曲，在学界内外都颇为常见。

2012 年，美国保守党政治家米特·罗姆尼＊在耶路撒冷演讲，援引戴蒙德的著作来支撑自己的观点，认为以色列与巴勒斯坦的工业发展差异是由文化差异所致。这也是罗姆尼另一观点的关键所在，他认为美国的保守文化是美国物质与军事成功最重要的原因。戴蒙德在《纽约时报》发文回应，称罗姆尼误解了他的观点。[6]

面对学界的质疑，戴蒙德认为这些批评并非基于他所收集的依据，而是出于道德理由。例如，他认为《质疑崩溃》的作者"偏好对人性的积极解读，因而质疑我对过往社会衰落的理解"。[7]他们"不接受我的观点，认为其说明的不过是'地理上的巧合'，……（而我的观点）以环境因素为基础，比如各大陆在生物地理禀赋[*]、形状、位置等方面的差异。但他们也没有提出自己的论点来替代我的。"[8]（"生物地理禀赋"指特定时间特定地域动植物的物种分布。）

虽然戴蒙德承认一些社会颇具复原力，得以在极端危机中生存下来（《质疑崩溃》力推这一观点），但他批评其他作者没有恰当地阐释这一观点。"例如，有一章写道，'格陵兰岛的诺尔斯人并未消亡，而是移居他国'，尽管没有证据表明其曾移居，却有关于饥荒的翔实考古证据——在格陵兰岛西殖民地最后一个冬天的考古地层最上层发现了骨头和残骸，证明发生了饥荒。"[9]

关于事实证据和研究方法的争论未有任何结果，此类情况实属罕见。同时，人类学界也落下了"刻意抨击戴蒙德"的名声。[10]

---

1. 戴维·科雷亚："去你的，贾雷德·戴蒙德"，《资本主义、自然、社会主义》第 24 卷，2013 年第 4 期，第 1—6 页。

2. 企鹅阅读指南,"对话贾雷德·戴蒙德",penguin.com,日期未注明,登录日期 2015 年 9 月 9 日,www.penguin.com/read/book-clubs/collapse/9780143117001。

3. 科雷亚:"去你的,贾雷德·戴蒙德",第 4 页。

4. 可参见:托尼·克鲁克,"土著人权",《今日人类学》第 14 卷,1998 年第 1 期,第 18—19 页。

5. 亚历克斯·戈卢布,"权力的游戏与人类学",《野性心灵》,2014 年 7 月 2 日,登录日期 2015 年 9 月 10 日,http://savageminds.org/2014/07/02/game-of-thrones-and-anthropology/。

6. 贾雷德·M. 戴蒙德:"罗姆尼没做功课",《纽约时报》,2012 年 8 月 1 日,登录日期 2015 年 9 月 30 日,www.nytimes.com/2012/08/02/opinion/mitt-romneys-search-for-simple-answers.html。

7. 贾雷德·M. 戴蒙德:"崩溃的两种观点",《自然》第 463 卷,2010 年 2 月 18 日第 7283 期,第 880 页。

8. 戴蒙德:"崩溃的两种观点",第 880 页。

9. 戴蒙德:"崩溃的两种观点",第 880 页。

10. 杰森·安特罗西奥:"贾雷德·戴蒙德与未来大众人类学",livinganthropologically.com,2014 年 7 月 21 日,登录日期 2015 年 9 月 10 日,www.livinganthropologically.com/2014/07/21/jared-diamond-future-public-anthropology/。

11 当代印迹

要点 ⚷━

- 对于喜欢人类历史宏大叙事的读者，《大崩溃》是不容错过的重要著作。然而，读者应当了解该书所引发的激烈辩论。

- 人类学、考古学、历史学、地理学等诸多学科的讨论都援引了《大崩溃》中的观点，但该书很少能帮助解决任何争议。

- 关于《大崩溃》，学者能达成的唯一共识是该书颇受大众欢迎，这得益于戴蒙德的科普才能。该书的大众影响力无可争议。

地位

贾雷德·M.戴蒙德的《大崩溃：社会如何选择兴亡》广泛吸引了喜欢历史鸿篇的人，但读者也应了解《大崩溃》及戴蒙德的类似著作所引发的辩论。关于《大崩溃》，众说纷纭，对书中观点的争议可分为以下几类：事实确凿与证据不足之间的争议；研究方法扎实与理论支持不足之间的争议；政治正确与道德不容之间的争议，而《大崩溃》的道德和政治立场尤其具有争议。

社会科学家对于《大崩溃》有一种普遍解读："戴蒙德关于社会消失和边缘化的说法是征服者的一大利器。"[1] 以及"《大崩溃》关注本土环境管理不善的案例，暗示'穷国'陷入贫困是因其'选择'逾越环境上限，因而导致崩溃。"[2]

戴蒙德曾明确表示，自己并不赞同上述道德或政治立场。他宣称撰写《枪炮、病菌与钢铁》是为说服西方人，使其意识到欧洲的统治并非由于种族优越。他想表明，西方的繁荣至少在一定程度上有赖于除了意志或种族优势之外的因素。

戴蒙德在《大崩溃》中再次强调环境因素，以此说明任何种族因素方面的解释都不够充分。他也强调个人行为十分重要，将更多责任置于人类本身（如在多米尼加共和国的案例中，拉斐尔·特鲁希略和华金·巴拉格尔推行环境预防政策）。

> "……完整列出潜在相关的所有变量，形成的模型十分复杂、难以理清，而戴蒙德的优点在于化繁为简。"
>
> ——约翰·R.麦克尼尔："可用的过去"

互动

与戴蒙德的其他著作一样，《大崩溃》也引发了诸多学科的讨论，尤其是人类学、考古学、历史学和地理学。然而争论双方难以达成一致，而且由于戴蒙德与批评者的观点无法调和，争论往往气竭力衰、无疾而终。

例如，有关《大崩溃》观点背后事实证据的讨论逐渐消退，因为双方都无法证明自己的历史解读和证据运用优于对方。《质疑崩溃》的作者认为，新墨西哥州的查科峡谷从未有过森林，因此当地的阿纳萨齐人不可能砍伐不曾存在的东西。他们进一步指出，分析当地林鼠贝丘*（啮齿动物堆积的排泄物）中的植物残余，"发现当时的气候和生态与当今几乎一样。"[3] 而戴蒙德则坚持认为，"利用放射性碳定年法分析贝丘发现，峡谷中原有的一片矮松与杜松混合林不见了。"[4] 可见，戴蒙德与批评者都提出了自己的论点和证据，互不相容。如此，再加上立场不可调和，争论往往陷入僵局。

有关环境决定论的争论也正因双方毫无共识而停滞不前。例如，历史学家指责戴蒙德没有充分考虑个人决策与机遇所带来的偶然影响。戴蒙德则指责历史学家否认环境因素对文化特征的作用。[5]

尽管多数争论都发生在专家圈内，但《大崩溃》对公众讨论同样有着不可否认的影响力。读者并不关心专家辩论，但对诸多主题兴趣渐浓，比如气候变化、环境破坏、文化相对论（认为解读个人行为时考虑其文化背景至关重要），以及从人类社会的不同命运中学习的可能性。[6]

尽管有其裨益，但也可认为，戴蒙德之所以招致众多专家质疑，正是因为他坚持面向大众读者写作。

持续争议

围绕《大崩溃》和戴蒙德其他著作的辩论持续不断，而争论焦点不断变化。有些批评者更多针对戴蒙德理论背后的支撑材料，有些关注《大崩溃》的道德与政治含意，有些则针对该书的理论价值。然而，多数辩论由于双方都缺乏确凿证据而无所进展，可以说是因为争论的实质基础本身具有缺陷。批评者讽刺戴蒙德，但他们也"受人嘲讽，被安进了诸多'你只是……'的套路句式中"：

- 你只是生气，因为戴蒙德不是人类学家。
- 你只是嫉妒，因为戴蒙德很受欢迎。
- 你只是个吹毛求疵的专家——戴蒙德则是个想法宏大的人。
- 你只是循规蹈矩的学者——戴蒙德则是智者。
- 你只是称戴蒙德为决定论者，然而他并不是。[7]

无论是因为对专业水平的嫉妒、对过度简化的指责，还是因为进一步事实证据的缺乏、思想认识的偏好，抑或是因为相冲突的理论立场，这些争论仍然悬而未决。

尽管如此，学者一致认为《大崩溃》与戴蒙德的其他著作一样，产生了极大的社会影响。这主要得益于戴蒙德的写作风格，即便其批评者也承认，戴蒙德的写作风格吸引了一批原本与科学话题有距离感的读者。受戴蒙德引人入胜、平易近人的风格的启发，一些人类学家也开始"试图缩小大众读者与科学间的距离"，[8] 让自己的写作更为通俗易懂。

1. 迈克·威尔科克斯："推行征服与消失的印第安人：从土著的角度回应贾雷德·戴蒙德在美国西南部的考古研究"，载《质疑崩溃：人类复原力、生态脆弱与帝国的未来》，帕特里夏·麦卡纳尼和诺曼·约菲编，纽约州纽约：剑桥大学出版社，2010 年，第 138 页。

2. 詹姆斯·L. 弗莱克斯纳："质疑崩溃：人类复原力、生态脆弱与帝国的未来"，《太平洋事务》第 84 卷，2011 年第 4 期，第 741 页。

3. 贾雷德·M. 戴蒙德："崩溃的两个观点"，《自然》第 463 卷，2010 年第 7283 期，第 880—881 页。

4. 戴蒙德："崩溃的两个观点"，第 881 页。

5. 贾雷德·M. 戴蒙德："地理决定论：'地理决定论'究竟意味着什么？"，jareddiamond.org，日期未注明，登录日期 2015 年 9 月 30 日，www.jareddiamond.org/Jared_Diamond/Geographic_determinism.html。

6. 马克·莱纳斯："复活节岛之谜——贾雷德·戴蒙德的回应"，marklynas.org，2011 年 9 月 22 日，登录日期 2015 年 9 月 10 日，www.marklynas.org/2011/09/the-myths-of-easter-island-jared-diamond-responds/。

7. 杰森·安特罗西奥："贾雷德·戴蒙德不会打败米特·罗姆尼——人类政治学 2012"，livinganthropologically.com，2012 年 8 月 4 日，登录日期 2015 年 9 月 10 日，www.livinganthropologically.com/2012/08/04/diamond-romney/。

8. 麦卡纳尼和约菲：《质疑崩溃》。另见：杰里米·麦克兰西和克里斯·麦克多诺编：《普及人类学》，伦敦：劳特利奇出版社，2002 年。

12 未来展望

要点 🔑

- 贾雷德·戴蒙德所著的《大崩溃》一书全球闻名，描述了不同时期世界各地诸多社会的情况。人类学家也越发渴望能产生如此大的影响力。他们再也无法忽视和否认，社会崩溃这样复杂的问题已成功在大众中普及的事实。

- 其他学者不太可能模仿戴蒙德的学术风格；大部分学者依然注重学科的复杂性多于平易近人的风格（这也可以解释为何多数学者的著作无法影响更广泛的受众）。

- 《大崩溃》提出的观点关乎全人类，如此宏大的理论吸引了广大受众，但也遭到专家的质疑。

潜力

全球畅销书《大崩溃：社会如何选择兴亡》由普利策奖得主贾雷德·M.戴蒙德所著，被译成几十种语言。该书甚至拍成了纪录片，由国家地理学会*在美国制作。该书修订版增加了关于柬埔寨吴哥的章节，于 2011 年出版。

不可否认，《大崩溃》对社会崩溃的研究以及有关气候变化和环境破坏的社会辩论都产生了影响。它很可能会保持自身的地位和影响力，并可能会影响未来的学术研究与公众讨论，尤其因为该书清晰展现了戴蒙德研究人类重大问题的方法所能产生的影响力。

但是，《大崩溃》并没呈现新的数据和研究方法，而是扩大了先前存在的案例研究的范围，整合出人类历史跨度最大的案例分析，并提出关乎全人类的理论观点。该书展现了戴蒙德成功的公式：一个关乎全人类的清晰问题，比较研究法，以及简洁明了的答案。归根结底，正因上述公式广受欢迎，戴蒙德的著作才能持续受到关注，尽管也引起了诸多争议。

戴蒙德的方法令其著作大获成功、广为人知、经久不衰。我们可以预见，这种方法将运用于未来的著作中以求类似的效果。在许多学科中，例如人类学领域，学者已经开始思考如何向戴蒙德学习，从而令自己的著作在公众领域广受推崇，具有意义。

例如，2013年美国人类学学会组织了一次专家讨论会，人类学家探讨了外行对于戴蒙德著作的接受程度，及其对公众讨论的影响力。由此可见，学界正在变化。人类学家日益意识到尽管他们"骇然于贾雷德·戴蒙德式的人类学，但它示范了如何让本科水平的读者了解人类学和世界历史。"[1] 不可否认，戴蒙德的著作如今是"民众认为自己了解文化与文化相对论（解读个人行为和信仰时，必须考虑其文化背景）知识的主要渠道。"[2] 因此，人类学家认为，"无视戴蒙德，或者……无视塑造戴蒙德的结构方法，都不是长久之计。"[3]

> "是的，还会有一本书，又是一本大部头，讨论人类历史和社会的另一个重大问题。我希望5年左右能写完。但是，正如柯南·道尔安排福尔摩斯向华生解释苏门答腊巨鼠之谜那样，'为时尚早，世界还没准备好听这个故事。'"
>
> —— 企鹅阅读指南，"对话贾雷德·戴蒙德"

未来方向

戴蒙德能令学术主题更通俗易懂、广为人知，《大崩溃》便是一个范例。人文与社会科学学者若想产生社会影响，或许会想要参考《大崩溃》。社会科学家日益意识到这种方法的重要意义，如英国一家研究质量评估机构——"研究卓越框架"便以对"经济、社会、公共政策、文化和生活品质"的影响为主要的评估标准。

尽管《大崩溃》展现了如何令社会科学在公众讨论中更受关注，但其他学者不太可能模仿戴蒙德的学术风格。社会科学家往往反对基于广泛比较得出结论的学者。人类学家尤其如此，他们否定得出简单答案的可能性，并强调社会文化现实十分复杂。[4]

然而，人类学家托马斯·许兰·埃里克森*写道："在当代人类学中，呼吁采用叙事手法几乎已是陈词滥调……但真正讲故事的人少之又少，这大概是这个学科普遍的职业弊病。"[5]相反，"戴蒙德便有讲故事的天赋。"[6]人类学家承认，讲故事和讲好故事，这也是人类古老和独有的渴望。[7]尽管人类学家努力解决复杂性与叙事之间的显著矛盾，但尚且无人能如戴蒙德般广受欢迎。

小结

《大崩溃》一经出版，几天内便成为畅销书，随后被制作成纪录片，在学界内外引起讨论。尽管该书的观点、研究方法和理论影响都遭到质疑，更勿论其政治和道德立场，但该书广受欢迎，这一点无人质疑。

其实，正因《大崩溃》在学界以外广受欢迎，才在专家中激起了诸多批评。《大崩溃》提出的人类社会命运观点关乎全人类。此类宏大的理论能吸引公众，却极少获得持怀疑态度的专家的支持。

《大崩溃》受大众欢迎的另一原因是戴蒙德所使用的比较研究

法。然而，无论这一方法如何吸引非专业人士，许多当代学者认为该方法并不恰当，因其过于看重相似点，而低估了不同点。

然而，无论你是否赞同戴蒙德的观点，其著作的影响力仍无可争议。

1. 杰森·安特罗西奥："贾雷德·戴蒙德与未来大众人类学"，livinganthropologically.com，2014 年 7 月 21 日，登录日期 2015 年 9 月 10 日，www.livinganthropologically.com/2014/07/21/jared-diamond-future-public-anthropology/。
2. 安特罗西奥："贾雷德·戴蒙德"。
3. 安特罗西奥："贾雷德·戴蒙德"。
4. 安特罗西奥："贾雷德·戴蒙德"。
5. 托马斯·H.埃里克森：《从事人类学：如何走入公众视野》，英国牛津、美国纽约州纽约：伯格出版社，2006 年。
6. 布林·威廉姆斯："能否相信贾雷德·戴蒙德？"，《石板书》，2013 年 2 月 18 日，登录日期 2015 年 9 月 30 日，www.slate.com/articles/health_and_science/books/2013/02/jared_diamond_the_world_until_yesterday_anthropologists_are_wary_of_lack.html。
7. 帕特里夏·A.麦卡纳尼和诺曼·约菲编：《质疑崩溃：人类复原力、生态脆弱与帝国的未来》，纽约州纽约：剑桥大学出版社，2010 年，第 1 页。

术语表

1. **阿纳萨齐**：源于纳瓦霍语的一个术语，指代旧时的阿纳萨齐人，其领土包括现在的犹他州南部、亚利桑那州北部、新墨西哥州西北部及科罗拉多州西南部。现普遍认为阿纳萨齐人的起源可以追溯至公元前 12 世纪。戴蒙德在《大崩溃》中列举出了公元 12 至 15 世纪之间阿纳萨齐不同群体及文化的衰落。

2. **人类学**：对人类的研究。分为多个子领域，每个子领域都聚焦于一个特定方面，如文化、社会制度、语言、生物学和经济等。

3. **考古学**：指通过对化石、文物和环境变动来研究过往的人类活动。

4. **价值论**：有关价值的理论，即特定群体认为有价值的所有事物。在戴蒙德所研究的社会背景中，一个社会的价值观决定了该社会群体克服大崩溃的能力。

5. **生物多样性**：测量特定生态系统中生物（动物和植物）的数量和种类的指标。生物多样性在全球范围内各不相同，并决定了各地居民的各种优势。例如，更丰富的生物多样性会增加饲料产量、作物产量和木材产量。

6. **生物地理禀赋**：特定时间与地理空间内植物和动物物种的分布。

7. **生物物理学**：一门利用物理学方法研究生物系统（如人体）的学科。

8. **植物学**：对植物的科学研究。

9. **酋邦**：独立的政治组织，该组织中个人地位由其所属的血统决定，根据其与最高酋长的亲属关系划分等级。

10. **气候**：气象变量长期和大规模的变化模式，这些变量包括温度、降水、风和湿度。气候与天气不同，天气是相对较小的地点范围内气象变量短期的变化模式。

11. **气候变化**：指气候长期、大规模的波动，比如数十年的干旱，一个世纪的潮湿天气，或 17 至 19 世纪的小冰期。戴蒙德在《大崩溃》中反复使用这一术语，如今通常用以指代"灾难性人为（人类主导）的全球变暖"。然而，气候变化并非仅由人类引起，自然环境变化也是原因之一。气候变化不一定会导致气候变暖，也可能使气候更冷、更潮湿、更干燥，更多变或不易变。

12. **比较环境史**：戴蒙德用该术语指代一种研究人类社会的方法，包括深入比较不同社会的案例研究，从而分离出能提供一般性解释的关键变量。

13. **比较研究法**：一种研究与分析方法，研究两个或多个案例，找到可能解释各自结果的相似点与不同点。

14. **大陆轴线**：一条假想线，若一片大陆领土的东西向距离长于南北向距离，则该线水平横跨该大陆。反之亦然，若一片大陆领土的南北向距离长于东西向距离，则该线垂直纵跨该大陆。

15. **文化帝国主义**：主导群体把其文化强加于被主导群体之上。文化帝国主义有多种形式，从军事控制到思想灌输。

16. **文化可能论**：一种地理学理论，认为文化由社会而非环境条件所塑造。因此，文化可能论的方法直接与地理决定论相对立。

17. **森林砍伐**：砍伐一片领土上的树木。砍伐森林的主要原因是农业，包括自给农业、商业农业和伐木业。

18. **生态学**：对生物与其栖息地之间关系的科学研究。生态学家倡导通过改变公共政策和个人行为来对环境资源进行可持续管理。

19. **经验主义**：一种知识理论，该理论认为直接观察是获得可靠知识的唯一方法。

20. **环境退化**：因资源逐渐枯竭导致的生态系统恶化。环境退化会导致空气和水枯竭、土壤质量退化以及野生动物灭绝。

21. **环境决定论**：该理论认为环境决定特定领土中社会的历史轨迹（路径）。环境决定论的极端观点认为，个人行为不能大幅改变环境因素对社会命运的影响，如气候、动物（群）、植物（群）和大陆地理轴线的影响。

22. **环境史学**：对人类社会与环境之间关系的科学研究。

23. **侵蚀**：土壤和岩石从一个地方到另一个地方的移动，由雨、风、农业及森林砍伐等因素引起。侵蚀的一大后果是土壤退化，这反过来又降低了土壤肥力。

24. **民族中心主义**：倾向于采用自身的文化理论与价值观来审视和评估其他民族的文化。通常，民族中心主义意味着自身所属的文化在某种程度上优于其他民族的文化。

25. **人种志**：对人类族群的科学研究，包括其风俗、习惯和信仰。

26. **地理决定论**：见"环境决定论"。

27. **全球化**：世界上人与人之间日益紧密连接的过程，其特点是越来越快速和频繁的旅行、通讯及物资交换。

28. **硬科学**：一种通俗的表达方式，通常用于指代自然科学或物理科学。化学、生物学与物理学等学科属于"硬科学"，因其使用假设和实验的方法理解宇宙。

29. **臃肿**：这一术语源自医学，表示系统或结构的过度增长。

30. **特殊规律研究**：指任何现象都不可比。特殊规律研究鼓励对具体属性的描述，而非对一般概念或规则的抽象总结。

31. **保守主义**：没有能力或不愿意采取政治行动，往往是价值观保守的结果。

32. **自变量**：这一术语源自数学，用于指代现象的外部原因。

33. **跨学科**：在一项研究活动中对不同学科的结合应用。与多学科不同的是，跨学科将多个学科综合成一种新的研究活动，而非通过许多单独的研究成果来解决特定的研究问题。

34. **实验室条件**：科学研究中不受外部干扰的可控条件。

35. **小冰期**：地球气候历史中的一个时期，自公元 1400 至 1800 年。在此期间，北半球的平均气温大幅下降。

36. **马尔萨斯陷阱**：由英国经济学家和人口统计学家托马斯·马尔萨斯提出，该理论认为，人口呈指数的增长往往会快于粮食产量的增长。

37. **贝丘**：在特定地点遗留下的古代废物。这些遗骸、粪便和其他各种旧物质对研究过往社会的考古学家十分有用。

38. **多发性原因**：一个事实由相互关联的多种原因造成。例如，戴蒙德的理论记述了多发性原因，因为该理论给出了导致社会崩溃的五个相互关联的因素。

39. **多学科**：当一门学科只能部分解决或描述复杂问题时，使用涉及多学科研究成果的方法。

40. **《国家地理》**：美国国家地理学会的杂志，自 1888 年起持续发行。

41. **自然实验**：观察一个环境（如某一领土的一群人）时，调查者无法控制该环境所受到的影响，并试图在外部干扰与研究对象的变化之间建立因果关系。

42. **一般性规律研究**：可以从一系列特定事实中概括出一般概念或规律。术语"一般规律的"通常与"特殊规律的"相对立。

43. **鸟类学**：关于鸟类的系统化的科学研究。

44. **人均收入**：衡量个人在某一地区平均收入的方式，通过将该地区的总收入除以总人口计算得出。

45. **光合能力**：地球上每英亩能够吸收的日照量。无论太阳产生的光量有多少，地球能吸收的光量都有一个最大值。这意味着，如果人类活动区域吸收掉大部分阳光，那么自然生态系统就没有太多剩余阳光可吸收。

46. **生理学**：生物学的一个分支学科，研究生物体的正常功能。

47. **花粉和木炭分析**：通过分析植物残余来测定某些植物在特定区域是

否存在的方法。

48. **博学家**：拥有多种兴趣及深入了解多种学科的人。通常，博学家会将理论知识与实践知识相结合，并且能说多种语言、演奏许多乐器。

49. **后古典时期**：中美洲历史上从公元 950 至 1539 年的时期。

50. **前哥伦布时期的玛雅文明**：公元前 2000 年前发展的中美洲文明，存在于墨西哥东南部、危地马拉、伯利兹、萨尔瓦多西部与洪都拉斯。该文明崩溃的部分原因是砍伐树木导致不可逆转的毁林现象，继而造成干旱。干旱又改变了当地的水循环，使降雨减少，从而引发持续干旱。

51. **放射性碳定年法**：通过分析一个物体所含的放射性碳来测定物体年代的方法，放射性碳即碳的放射性同位素。由于在动植物死亡后，其体内放射性碳的含量会不断减少，因此能通过这一方法大致计算动物或植物何时死亡。

52. **重新造林**：曾遭遇森林砍伐的地区，由于人类有意种植或树木自然生长而产生的每英亩存活树木数量增加。

53. **复原力**：一个机制（如社会或生物体）能应对变化和挑战的能力。例如，气候复原力指生态环境或人类社会适应温度与湿度长期变化的能力。

54. **卢旺达**：非洲中东部的赤道国家。1994 年 4 至 7 月，卢旺达发生了对大约 50 至 100 万人的大屠杀，其中数量最多的是图西族人，死于胡图族人手中。

55. **盐渍化**：土壤中盐含量的增加。盐渍化的后果包括植物生长迟缓、产量减少、水质下降，以及土壤侵蚀增加。

56. **社会达尔文主义**：一系列理论，解释进化论、自然选择与适者生存等相关人类现象。社会达尔文主义源于查尔斯·达尔文的自然选择理论，该理论最初并不旨在被用于探讨社会文化问题。种族主义与帝国主义观点认为自然造就"胜利者"和"失败者"，这种观点的批评者创造了"社会达尔文主义"这一术语。

57. **可持续性**：能够利用环境资源而不耗尽环境资源或破坏环境。

58. **日本德川幕府时期**：指日本历史上由德川幕府统治社会的时期，德川幕府是从 1603 至 1868 年统治日本的封建军政府。

59. **水资源管理**：能够使用水资源而不耗尽水资源、降低水质量或破坏环境。

60. **西方帝国主义**：大致指为欧洲大国统治非洲、大洋洲及美洲大陆大面积领土辩护的意识形态。这种辩护通常带有种族主义色彩，认为控制和管理这些大陆的，不应是当地居民，而是因具有种族优势而能做得更好的人。

人名表

1. 亚里士多德（公元前384—前322），古希腊雅典柏拉图学院的哲学家和科学家。他阐明了因不同气候情况而引起的北欧人、亚洲人和希腊人之间的文化差异。

2. 保罗·巴恩，英国考古学家、翻译家、作家和广播员，围绕一系列考古问题广泛著书，包括《复活节岛之谜》（与约翰·弗伦利合著，2003）。

3. 华金·巴拉格尔（1906—2002），多米尼加共和国1960年至1996年期间的三届（非连任）总统。

4. 弗朗茨·博厄斯（1859—1942），人类学家，出生于普鲁士，被称为"美国人类学之父"。博厄斯反对通过进化方法研究文化，提倡历史特殊论和文化相对论。

5. 马克·布伦纳，湖沼学家和古湖沼学家（研究河流、湖泊等水体），对热带及亚热带的湖泊和分水岭有特殊兴趣。布伦纳基于湖泊底部的沉积物柱芯重建了水生生态系统的历史。

6. 戴维·科雷亚（1968年生），美国学者和活动家，新墨西哥大学美国研究副教授。

7. 乔治·考吉尔（1929—2018），美国人类学家和考古学家，具有墨西哥特奥蒂瓦坎实地工作经验。考吉尔出版了大量著作，对古代国家和城市的比较研究作出贡献。

8. 贾森·H.柯蒂斯，佛罗里达大学地球化学领域的高级顾问，古代社会气候变异方面的专家。

9. 托马斯·许兰·埃里克森（1962年生），挪威奥斯陆大学社会人类学教授，现任欧洲社会人类学家协会主席。埃里克森的一大研究兴趣是普及社会人类学。

10. 弗雷德里克·K.埃林顿，三一学院的人类学荣誉教授，在巴布亚新几内亚、苏门答腊和蒙大拿州有研究经验，大部分工作都是与妻子德博拉·格维尔茨合作完成。

11. **布莱恩·费根**（1936年生），考古学家和人类学家，拥有非洲实地工作经验。

12. **约翰·弗伦利**，新西兰梅西大学生物地理学荣誉教授，孢粉学家（"灰尘"——花粉和花粉孢子——研究专家）。弗伦利在古孢粉学领域著作等身。

13. **亚历克斯·戈卢布**，巴布亚新几内亚人类学家，具有实地工作经验。戈卢布是大众文化人类学网站"savageminds.org"的创始人，该网站与贾雷德·戴蒙德的工作息息相关。

14. **希波克拉底**（公元前460—前370），被称为"西方医学之父"，认为环境是塑造人类性格、身体和文化主要特征的原因。

15. **戴维·A.霍德尔**（1958年生），地质学家和古气候学家，剑桥大学地质学教授。霍德尔与布伦纳、柯蒂斯和吉尔德森主要关注玛雅帝国的崩溃。

16. **特里·亨特**，考古学家，俄勒冈大学人类学教授，研究重点是环境变化和太平洋岛屿上的生活，在太平洋考古学、史前史和语言学领域发表了大量成果。

17. **卡尔·利波**，考古学家，曾研究密西西比河谷的史前陶工和复活节岛上著名的摩艾石像建造。

18. **马塞尔·莫斯**（1872—1950），法国社会学家，因出版人类学著作《礼物》（1925）而闻名，该著作对比了不同物体在过去和当前社会中的流通。

19. **帕特里夏·A.麦卡纳尼**（1953年生），北卡罗来纳大学人类学凯南杰出教授，曾在玛雅地区开展考古研究，目前与当代玛雅社区一起开展遗产项目。

20. **邦妮·J.麦凯**，罗格斯大学人类学荣誉退休教授。

21. 托马斯·麦戈文，环境和岛屿考古学及气候变化领域教授。

22. 约翰·罗伯特·麦克尼尔（1954 年生），乔治城大学环境史教授，其最有名的著作是《阳光下的新事物：20 世纪世界环境史》（2000）。

23. 孟德斯鸠（1689—1755），法国律师兼政治哲学家，在《论法的精神》中，孟德斯鸠认为气候可能对人类和社会产生重大影响。

24. 迪克·皮特（1940 年生），克拉克大学人文地理学教授，《对极》期刊创始人，主要从事政治和生态学工作。

25. 本尼·派泽（1957 年生），利物浦约翰摩尔斯大学的社会人类学家，全球变暖政策基金会主任。

26. 柏拉图（公元前 424—前 348），哲学家和数学家，苏格拉底的学生，一些人视其为"哲学之父"。

27. 威廉·里斯（1943 年生），不列颠哥伦比亚大学教授，研究兴趣涉及全球环境趋势、气候变化和社会经济可持续发展。

28. 詹姆斯·鲁滨逊（1960 年生），经济学家和政治科学家，目前担任芝加哥大学教授，与达龙·阿西莫格鲁共同撰写了《为何国家会失败：权力、繁荣与贫困的起源》（2012），与贾雷德·戴蒙德共同撰写了《历史的自然实验》（2010）。

29. 米特·罗姆尼（1947 年生），美国商人和共和党政治家，2012 年 11 月的总统大选中，被民主党总统巴拉克·奥巴马击败。

30. 克莱尔·拉塞尔（1919—1999），心理治疗师和诗人，威廉·M. S. 拉塞尔的妻子。克莱尔与丈夫一起工作，就精神分析、动物行为、古代文明崩溃等多种主题发表著作。

31. 威廉·M. S. 拉塞尔（1925—2006），雷丁大学荣誉教授，与妻子合著《希腊和罗马的神话》（2000）和《人口危机与人口周期》（1999）。

32. 卡尔·奥尔特温·索尔（1889—1975），美国加州大学伯克利分校的地理学荣誉教授，索尔对该学科最重要贡献之一是他对环境决定论的坚定批评。

33. 约瑟夫·泰恩特（1949 年生），美国人类学家和历史学家，因著作《复杂社会的崩溃》（1988）而闻名，该书对比了玛雅、查科和罗马帝国的崩溃。

34. 拉斐尔·特鲁希略（1891—1961），1930 年至 1961 年多米尼加共和国的统治者，其执政风格以自上而下的暴力和镇压为特征。然而，特鲁希略带来了一个普遍稳定和经济繁荣的时代。

35. 安德鲁·P. 韦达（1931 年生），罗格斯大学人类学和生态学荣誉教授，《人类生态学》学术期刊创始人。

36. 迈克·V. 威尔科克斯，斯坦福大学人类学副教授，其专业领域包括美国西南部的文化和考古学，其出版物批评了戴蒙德的著作。

37. 诺曼·约菲（1944 年生），亚述学家（分析古代近东亚述帝国的学者）和人类学家，从对比的视角研究并发表了关于古巴比伦时期和古代国家兴衰的成果。

WAYS IN TO THE TEXT

- Jared M. Diamond is a polymath* scholar—possessing a depth of knowledge in many fields of interest—whose work combines various parallel interests with an accessible narrative style. His approach has won him considerable if controversial fame across the world.

- Published in 2005, *Collapse: How Societies Choose to Fail or Survive* argues that societies fail because of five key factors; societies in many parts of the world today will also collapse, he argues, unless they learn lessons from those that survived.

- *Collapse* matters because it deals with global environmental issues and general patterns in human history, and because it has generated debate among academics.

Who Is Jared M. Diamond?

Jared M. Diamond, the author of *Collapse: How Societies Choose to Fail or Survive* (also sometimes subtitled *How Societies Choose to Fail or Succeed*), was born in 1937 in Boston, Massachusetts. His parents—his father was a pediatrician, his mother a teacher and concert pianist—were of Eastern European Jewish origin. Since his early years he has directed his inquisitive mind in multiple directions. For example, while his PhD at Cambridge University focused on the biophysics* and physiology* of membranes in the gall bladder (biophysics being the study of biological systems with methods borrowed from physics; physiology being the study of the functioning of living organisms),[1] he also conducted research in the ornithology* (study of birds) and ecology* (which examines the relationships between species and environment) of the South

Pacific island of New Guinea.

In 1968 he was appointed professor of physiology at the medical school of the University of California, Los Angeles (UCLA). However, it is his interdisciplinary* approach (drawing on different academic disciplines) that laid the basis for his successful career. Ornithology taught him the value of comparing different populations that live in similar environments, a technique he later combined with his third research interest, environmental history.* This combination of environmental history and comparative methods* (systems requiring the examination of two or more cases to identify similarities and differences that might explain their respective outcomes) became a trademark, which he popularized with an accessible and storytelling-like writing style.

The formula proved extremely successful. Before, he had published only—though prolifically—in the fields of physiology, ecology, and ornithology.[2] Then, in the 1990s, he became more widely known following the publication of his books written for a popular audience. After his award-winning *The Third Chimpanzee* (1991), he received several prizes for *Guns, Germs, and Steel* (1997), including a Pulitzer Prize for General Nonfiction. *Collapse* (2005) is his fourth book.

What Does *Collapse* Say?

In *Collapse*, Diamond asks why some past civilizations experienced a severe reduction in population and considerable decreases in political, economic, and social complexity, before eventually collapsing. His answer is that they fell victim to one or more of the following five key factors: environmental degradation* (the decline of an ecosystem as a result of the progressive depletion of its resources), including overpopulation; changes in the climate;* hostile neighbors; weakened trading partners; and an absence of the cultural resources that enable a society to tackle these and other problems. He supports this general conclusion with a comparison between a set of historical civilizations, including the pre-Columbian Maya* of Mesoamerica (specifically what is today southeastern Mexico, Guatemala, Belize, the western part of El Salvador, and Honduras), the Norse (medieval Scandinavian) colonies of Greenland, the Polynesians of Henderson, Pitcairn, and Easter Islands, and the Anasazi* people of the American Southwest (the ancient inhabitants of the territory comprising contemporary southern Utah, northern Arizona, northwestern New Mexico, and southwestern Colorado).

The five key factors combined in different ways depending on their number and mutual influence. For example, all five contributed to the inexorable decline of the Norse colonies. Four out of five destroyed the Maya (no role was played by trade partners), and only three caused the collapse of the Anasazi— deforestation* (the removal of trees), a protracted drought, and the failure to solve the ensuing societal problems.

Diamond suggests that these same factors may undermine contemporary global societies, too, and even destroy them. For example, one or more of the five factors caused the recent fall of the African nations of Somalia and Rwanda,* and the former Yugoslavia, and are currently threatening countries such as Iraq and Indonesia. Even Australia and the United States are at risk, particularly from environmental damage, which is probably the single greatest threat to societies across the world.

Just a single factor can initiate the downward spiral of collapse. It happened in Easter Island, in the southeastern Pacific, where massive deforestation inadvertently caused a chain reaction leading to ecological and civilizational self-destruction. Similarly, pollution caused by global industrial powers potentially risks unsustainable damage.

Hence, *Collapse* urges readers to become conscious of the importance of human activities in shaping the future of civilizations, and to take corrective action against upcoming environmental catastrophes.

In the search for practical lessons that might help us to deal with our own problems, Diamond again looks at past civilizations. He analyzes cases in Japan of the Tokugawa* period (1603–1868), the Pacific island of Tikopia, and the New Guinea Highlands, and infers that ecological catastrophes can be avoided with a combination of restraint, increased knowledge, and axiological* flexibility—the ability of any given society to change its cultural values.

In contrast, other societies "chose" not to ensure their long-term sustainability*, even if they were aware of their decline. For example, the Norse knew that their neighbors, the Inuit, were better able to cope with changes in the climate and other challenging factors. But their blind commitment to religion, their strong social cohesion, and their scorn for the Inuit (whom they regarded as inferior) prevented them from changing their values and learning from their neighbors. A similar kind of axiological rigidity, Diamond concludes, is also preventing contemporary global societies from making the choices that would promote *our* long-term sustainability.

Why Does *Collapse* Matter?

In *Collapse*, Diamond reaches conclusions that are relevant for one of the most controversial debates today: man-made climate change, its consequences, and the ways in which we should respond to it. In fact, he conceived the book precisely as an opportunity to learn from past societies that dealt with their environmental problems.

These preoccupations are motivated not only by the perceived risk of an upcoming catastrophe, but also by the lack of consensus regarding the extent and consequences of human-activated climate change. *Collapse* proves that such uncertainties and the ensuing political paralysis—immobilism*—is not new. There were societies in the past that, though aware of their decline, did not necessarily take steps to overcome it.

Indeed, Diamond contends that whether a society collapses or not largely depends on its cultural values and its political, economic, and social institutions. By producing factual evidence that human activities did change the course of distant societies, he intends to persuade us that our corrective action matters for us today just as much as it did for people in the past.

Unsurprisingly, *Collapse* proved an almost instant best seller and has been translated into 31 languages. Its success is clear evidence not just of the inherent and wide appeal of Diamond's subject matter, but of his talents as a popularizer of complex historical problems and their relevance to industrial societies today.

Readers appreciate not only the content of Diamond's work, but also his style of reasoning. With *Guns, Germs, and Steel*, a book based on the so-called "natural experiment"* (the study of a context exposed to influences beyond the control of the investigators, who try to demonstrate causal connections) and the comparison between societies that differ in time and space, he enjoyed similar strong sales. On the other hand, specialist academics around the world—especially anthropologists* (who study human beings), archaeologists* (who study past human activity), geographers, and historians—are very critical of these "popular" methodologies.

The ensuing controversy, however, proves that the book matters in the debate about how we can learn from previous societies. While specialists insist that there are irreducible differences between past and present, Diamond provides evidence that there are common elements, too. These commonalities are what make us human and, as such, they are of continuing relevance and importance.

---

1. Jared M. Diamond, "Concentrating Activity of the Gall-bladder" (PhD diss., University of Cambridge, 1961).

2. See, for example: Jared M. Diamond et al., "Geophagy in New Guinea Birds," *Ibis* 141, no. 2 (1999): 181–93.

SECTION 1
INFLUENCES

MODULE 1
THE AUTHOR AND THE HISTORICAL CONTEXT

KEY POINTS

- As in his previous work, in *Collapse* Diamond draws on the aims and methods of several academic disciplines to answer a question relevant for humanity at large: in this case, that of societal collapse.

- Diamond combined multiple interests, methods, and an accessible writing style into a unique blend that gained his books worldwide acclaim, notwithstanding much specialist criticism.

- Diamond's unique formula results from his career in physiology* (which looks at the functioning of biological systems) and ornithology* (the study of birds), his personal interest in anthropology* (which studies humankind) and the environment, and from his life experiences as a fieldworker and science writer.

Why Read This Text?

Jared M. Diamond's best-selling *Collapse: How Societies Choose to Fail or Survive* (2005) asks why some societies collapse and others do not. This is a typical "Diamondian" question, similar to the one he asked in his Pulitzer Prize-winning book *Guns, Germs, and Steel* (1997), where he asked why some societies come to dominate and others to be dominated. The way in which Diamond answers the question in *Collapse* is also typical of his argumentative style: a sweeping comparison between societies distant in space and time, observed as if they were "natural experiments"* (the observation of, say, a group of people in a given territory, exposed to influences beyond the control of the investigators, in order to establish causal connections between those influences and any changes observed). Diamond also explains *Collapse*'s appeal in relation to his previous book, writing that: "many people... were looking out for my next book, but the other reason is that the subject of *Collapse* really grabs people."[1]

The "subject of *Collapse*" is societal collapse defined as a "drastic decrease in human population size and/or political/ economic/social complexity, over a considerable area, for an extended time." This is a theme that Diamond had already addressed before the publication of *Collapse*.[2] In the book, he argues that different combinations of five factors caused and are causing the collapse of both past and present societies.

Diamond developed this intellectual style as an amalgamation of different disciplines he studied throughout his life. He began his intellectual career as a physiologist, developed a parallel interest in ornithology, then history, and eventually ethnography* (the study of groups of people, their customs, habits, and beliefs). His formula has been extremely successful, gaining him wide fame with his books written for a non-specialist audience. These include *The Third Chimpanzee* (1991),[3] *Guns, Germs, and Steel* (1997),[4] *The World Until Yesterday* (2012),[5] and *Why Is Sex Fun?* (1997),[6] *Collapse* is another milestone in this intellectual journey from the natural and physical sciences to social sciences and to popular science writing.

> *"Ever since I was in my 20s and read Thor Heyerdahl's books about Easter Island, I became intrigued by the collapse of great societies—as are millions of other people. That interest has stayed with me over the last forty years, stimulated by visits to Maya ruins and Anasazi sites and by reading about other collapsed societies. I did not conceive of* Guns, Germs, and Steel *and* Collapse *as companion volumes from the start, but... as soon as I came to think about what would be the subject of my next book, the answer became obvious:* Collapse!*"*
>
> —— Penguin Reader's Guide, "A Conversation with Jared Diamond"

Author's Life

In 1937 Jared M. Diamond was born in Boston, Massachusetts, to a couple of Eastern European Jewish origin. Like his mother, he studied piano and became interested in teaching. Presumably influenced by his father, a pediatrician—a doctor specializing in children—Diamond obtained a PhD from Cambridge University on the physiology of membranes in the gall bladder.

At the same time, he developed an interest in ornithology and ecology* (the relationship between species and environment). He conducted research on the birds and environment of the Pacific island of New Guinea, and started to publish his findings. About this part of his life, he said: "Luckily my [academic] papers about birds were published in journals which no gall bladder physiologists ever read... In academia, working in multiple fields is not a benefit but a penalty."[7]

Diamond developed a third line of investigation in environmental history* (the investigation of the relationship between human societies and the environment). He also began writing for a non-academic public. With his second book, *Guns, Germs, and Steel*, he achieved worldwide fame and was awarded a series of prizes. However, *Guns, Germs, and Steel* attracted fierce criticism, too. The book's conclusions gained him the reputation, among academics, of being a cultural imperialist* (one who imposes his or her own cultural values on others), an environmental determinist* (one who believes that the environment is the deciding factor for social outcomes), and a radical empiricist* (one who refuses to consider evidence that cannot be verified by observation).

In *Collapse*, Diamond seriously confronted those criticisms. Along with the radical empiricism of the natural experiment and the comparative method* (the analysis of different cases in order to identify similarities and differences that might explain differing outcomes), which he did not abandon, he enriched his research toolkit with the ethnographic methods of anthropology. It follows that his life has been underscored by a constant effort to answer general questions about humanity by blending the methods from different disciplines, notwithstanding the attacks of colleagues and critics.

Author's Background

Diamond's background deeply influenced his intellectual production. His doctoral studies in physiology convinced him of the value of isolating variables with the experimental method. He would later apply this method to study the history of relatively isolated societies, such as those of Tikopia and Easter Island in the Pacific. Later, his ornithological research in New Guinea required him to compare the environmental habitats of birds to understand the impact of a set of independent variables* (an expression borrowed from mathematics to indicate the external cause of a phenomenon). When he wrote his books, he used the same comparative methods to understand the evolution of human societies in relation to a set of independent variables—such as climate,* biodiversity,* fauna (animals), and continental axis.*

The intersection between experimental and comparative methods and Diamond's later interest in environmental history and in popularizing science resulted in his famous book *Guns, Germs, and Steel*. The book was widely acclaimed, but also made Diamond the target of much criticism, especially by anthropologists. In *Collapse*, Diamond tackles his critics head on by opening the book with a very ethnographic first chapter.

The chapter draws heavily on Diamond's own knowledge of Montana in the western United States. As a teenager, in the 1950s, he used to spend a few weeks of the summer in the state of Montana. His father prescribed medical treatment to a rancher's child, and a strong bond developed between the two families as a consequence.[8] Diamond later bought a house in Montana, which gave him even more opportunities to gain insights into the points of view of Montanans about the destiny of their territory.

Along with this insider perspective, in this chapter he

compares several case studies of water, air, and soil pollution, as well as other major problems afflicting Montana today. So he uses ethnography, natural experiment, and the comparative method again. In conclusion, *Collapse* is not only a comparison of different societies, but also a synthesis of methodologies that Diamond has been refining throughout his whole life.

1. Penguin Reader's Guide, "A Conversation with Jared Diamond," penguin. com, n.d., accessed September 9, 2015, www.penguin.com/read/book-clubs/collapse/9780143117001.

2. Jared M. Diamond, "The Last Americans: Environmental Collapse and the End of Civilization," *Harper's Magazine*, June 2003; Diamond, "Easter's End," *Discover Magazine*, August 1995; Diamond, "Paradise Lost," *Discover Magazine*, November 1997.

3. Jared M. Diamond, *The Third Chimpanzee: The Evolution and Future of the Human Animal* (London: HarperCollins, 2006).

4. Jared M. Diamond, *Guns, Germs, and Steel* (London: Random House, 2013).

5. Jared M. Diamond, *The World Until Yesterday: What Can We Learn from Traditional Societies?* (New York: Viking, 2013).

6. Jared M. Diamond, *Why Is Sex Fun?: The Evolution of Human Sexuality* (London: Hachette, 2014).

7. Gillian Tett, "The Science Interview: Jared Diamond," *Financial Times*, October 11, 2013, accessed September 30, 2015, www.ft.com/intl/cms/s/2/1f786618-307a-11e3-80a4-00144feab7de. html#axzz3jQUrhdub.

8. Jared M. Diamond, *Collapse: How Societies Choose to Fail or Survive* (London: Penguin, 2011), 27.

MODULE 2
ACADEMIC CONTEXT

KEY POINTS

* Diamond has not necessarily discovered something new. Rather, his innovation consists in analyzing and presenting existing material in novel ways.

* The study of the relationship between human societies and the environment began with a school of thought called "environmental determinism"* (the theory that the environment determines the historical trajectories of a society associated with a particular territory), with which Diamond is closely associated.

* In writing *Collapse*, Diamond was influenced by his predecessors to the extent that he used existing data on past collapses both to engage with and expand on previous theories of societal collapse.

The Work in Its Context

Before Jared M. Diamond's *Collapse: How Societies Choose to Fail or Survive* was published, the theme of societal collapse had been explored by the anthropologist* Norman Yoffee* and the anthropologist and archaeologist* George Cowgill,*[1] as well as by the archaeologist and anthropologist Brian Fagan,*[2] and the anthropologist and historian Joseph Tainter.*[3] In the 1990s, researchers became increasingly interested in accounting for societal collapse with environmental explanations. For example, in a 1995 article published in *Nature*, David A. Hodell,* Jason H. Curtis,* and Mark Brenner,* a team of researchers with different specialisms in the natural sciences, argued that a shift toward drier climate* conditions accelerated the collapse of the pre-Columbian Maya* people (a civilization that occupied the area of what is today southeastern Mexico, Guatemala, Belize, the western part of El Salvador, and Honduras from some 4,000 years ago).[4] It is from these studies that Diamond forms his synthesis in order to draw lessons for today.

The environmental historian John R. McNeill* explains that "environmental historians have normally resisted the urge" of "combing the past for episodes that provide salutary lessons for the present."[5] In contrast, Diamond proposes that history be considered as a science that produces laws, allows predictions, and can be instructive about current affairs. Even though it is impossible to create laboratory conditions* in these fields (unlike chemistry or physics), the so-called "natural experiment"* is possible. This consists of comparing different, non-laboratory-bound cases in which a potentially key variable is absent or present.

For example, you can note that Easter Island and Mayan societies collapsed while experiencing environmental damage. From this you can postulate that environmental damage is a major cause of collapse. However, a correlation between collapse and environment should be drawn while taking differences into account. In this case, it is determining that Easter Island was an isolated island in the middle of the Pacific, and that the Mayan Empire was anything but isolated or peripheral. This difference highlights that isolation is not a necessary condition for collapse but a dispensable cause.

> *"Most geographers think of the theory of environmental determinism as a musty, fusty relic of the past. But most geographers do not pay much attention to the best-seller lists."*
>
> ——James M. Blaut, "Environmentalism and Eurocentrism"

Overview of the Field

At the beginning of the twentieth century, environmental determinism was the prevailing theory in geography. It dates back to the thinkers of ancient Greece, such as the philosophers Plato* and Aristotle* and the physician Hippocrates,* and to later philosophers such as Montesquieu,* active in the eighteenth century, who asserted that environmental factors cause racial, cultural, social, and moral differences between populations. Environmental determinism can be summarized as follows: "Cold northern climates produce hardy and thrifty people" whereas "the unrelenting heat along the equator produces lazy people."[6]

Environmental determinism was opposed by the American geographer Carl O. Sauer* and other so-called "cultural possibilists"*[7] in the 1920s; for them, the approach reduced human beings to mere subjects of the environment, and was therefore unable to account for human modifications of the environment itself. They proposed, instead, a cultural perspective to understand the relationship between people and the environment. However, the application of these ideas was complicated by the controversial definition of culture, something that has been the subject of endless debate. Culture was initially considered to be synonymous with civilization; this idea was criticized for measuring all cultures from less to more civilized. So a new tendency to define each different culture according to its own values, beliefs, and practices emerged. In the search for unifying underlying principles, scholars later began to examine the elementary structures of each culture. Culture was looked at as a particular discourse from which it was possible to extract a sort of grammar. But this approach was seen as unable to account for human initiative and change. Ultimately, no single definition of culture is unanimously accepted.[8]

From the 1960s, culture was seen as the product of the systemic interaction between human beings and the environment (that is, the interactions inside a system defined, in this case, by people and the environment).[9] Then, the anthropologists Andrew P. Vayda* and Bonnie J. McCay* proposed a focus on individual behavior to identify the specific paths of systemic interactions.[10] Subsequently, a more structural approach was introduced to frame these individual paths within the broader setting of political and ideological forces.

These different perspectives are not discussed in *Collapse*. Rather than addressing a specific debate in the field of human—environment relationships, Diamond stepped into the discussion with a modified version of the environmental determinist position. Instead of explaining human societies as a mere consequence of their different environmental conditions, Diamond theorized a complex interlocking of multiple factors, including culture, politics, and even chance.

Academic Influences

Diamond was aware of previous attempts by other scholars to explain the causes of societal collapse. For example, in *The Collapse of Complex Societies* (1988), the anthropologist Joseph Tainter argues that societies collapse after reaching an unsustainable degree of complexity because they are unable to produce enough organizational and physical energy to support their hypertrophic*—excessively, unsustainably grown—structure.[11]

To reach this conclusion, Tainter compared three cases of collapse: the Western Roman Empire, the Maya civilization, and the Anasazi* culture of the southwestern United States, an approach that resembles Diamond's own comparative method. Tainter, however, concluded that collapse is a feature of all societies, whereas Diamond, on the basis of a larger sample of cases, argues that some societies avoid that kind of crisis.

Diamond is also familiar with "Population Crises and Population Cycles," a work by the British scholars William M. S. Russell* and Claire Russell,* who, like Tainter, argue that societies are structurally responsible for their crises.[12] Crises, for the Russells, depend on the differential growth of the population and the resources to support it. Societies can relieve the pressure of a growing population only with measures such as birth control. Examples recalled in this study are borrowed from China, West Africa, western Asia, the northern Mediterranean, and northwest Europe. Diamond himself mentions birth control as a prudent measure taken by the people of the southwest Pacific island of Tikopia to avoid the collapse of their society. However, he does not consider population growth as the only or main cause of societal collapse. Rather, his argument is that there are multiple causes, and that a major role is played by the environment.

These studies influenced Diamond to the extent that they

provided him with a larger set of case studies. In terms of theory, he does not necessarily argue against Tainter's theory that societies have a tendency to collapse. Rather, he makes the additional point that they can survive their crises if corrective measures are taken in time. Similarly, the theory that collapse is caused by the differential growth of a population and the resources to support it is actually part of Diamond's own reasoning about the collapse of the African state of Rwanda.*

---

1. Norman Yoffee and George Cowgill, eds., *The Collapse of Ancient States and Civilizations* (Tucson: University of Arizona Press, 1988).

2. Brian Fagan, *Floods, Famines, and Emperors: El Niño and the Fate of Civilizations* (New York: Basic Books, 1999).

3. Joseph Tainter, *The Collapse of Complex Societies* (Cambridge: Cambridge University Press, 1988).

4. David A. Hodell et al., "Possible Role of Climate in the Collapse of Classic Maya Civilization," *Nature* 375, no. 6530 (1995): 391–4.

5. John R. McNeill, "A Usable Past," *American Scientist* 93, no. 2 (2005): 172.

6. David Correia, "F**k Jared Diamond," *Capitalism Nature Socialism* 24, no. 4 (2013): 1–6.

7. Gabriel Judkins et al., "Determinism within Human-Environment Research and the Rediscovery of Environmental Causation," *The Geographical Journal* 174, no. 1 (2008): 17–29.

8. See: Tim Ingold, "Introduction to Culture," in *Companion Encyclopedia of Anthropology*, ed. Tim Ingold (London and New York: Routledge, 1994), 329–49.

9. Karl W. Butzer, "Cultural Ecology," in *Geography in America*, ed. Gary L. Gaile and Cort J. Willmott (Columbus: Merrill, 1989), 192–208; Marvin Harris, *Cultural Materialism: The Struggle for a Science of Culture* (New York: Random House, 1979); Roy A. Rappaport, *Pigs for the Ancestors: Ritual in the Ecology of a New Guinea People* (New Haven: Yale University Press,1968).

10. Andrew P. Vayda and Bonnie J. McCay, "New Directions in Ecology and Ecological Anthropology," *Annual Review of Anthropology* 4 (1975): 293–306.

11. Tainter, *Collapse of Complex Societies*.

12. Claire Russell and William M. S. Russell, "Population Crises and Population Cycles," *Medicine, Conflict and Survival* 16, no. 4 (2000): 383–410.

THE PROBLEM

KEY POINTS

- At the core of Diamond's works *Guns, Germs, and Steel* and *Collapse* are questions about the fate of human societies and of the right way to study the history of human societies.

- Participants in the debate criticize both *Collapse* and previous works by Diamond for similar reasons, including environmental determinism* (the belief that it is environment, exclusively, that decides society and social outcomes), and for blaming past civilizations for their own collapses.

- The contemporary debate is dominated by accusations of environmental determinism and Western imperialism* (the ideology justifying the rule of European powers over large territories in Africa, Oceania, and the Americas). Rather than questioning the overall conclusions of *Collapse*, participants in the discussion question Diamond's ideological, methodological, and theoretical approaches.

Core Question

At the core of Jared M. Diamond's *Collapse: How Societies Choose to Fail or Survive* is a question about the cause of all societal collapses. By comparing a series of modern and ancient case studies, Diamond argues that all societal collapses result from a combination of the same five factors. He proposes that modern societies collapse because they are unable to solve the same kind of problems faced by those in the past. Diamond intended this theory to be valid for all societies past, present, and future. He calls the method with which he achieved such a comprehensive theory "comparative environmental history."* This is the same kind of approach he used for his previous book *Guns, Germs, and Steel*.[1] It follows that *Collapse* is not only a book about societal failures but also a confirmation of Diamond's belief in this method.

Guns, Germs, and Steel was criticized for using this approach. Critics found it excessively simplistic to determine the fate of human societies in environmental terms. A more comprehensive explanation of the relationship between society and history, in their view, needs to take into account power relations and other human activities, rather than the supposedly all-encompassing influence of the environment.

In *Guns*, however, Diamond was not necessarily as simplistic as his critics argued. The title of the book itself listed three concurring causes; if he used the same kind of approach to answer the question posed in *Collapse* (that is, a multiplicity of factors and the prominent role played by the environment), it is because he was persuaded it was sound. It follows that at the core of *Collapse* there is not only a question about the fate of human societies but also a certain reaffirmation of Diamond's method for studying them.

> "Diamond won a Pulitzer Prize because he made this ridiculous, racist argument sound like common sense. His books do not merely sanitize a history of colonial violence; they are its disinfectant."
>
> —— David Correia, "F**k Jared Diamond"

The Participants

Theorists of societal collapse, such as the American anthropologist*
and historian Joseph Tainter* and the British scholars William M.
S.* and Claire Russell,* are among the main academic influences on
Collapse. Rather than arguing against or in favor of their theories,
Diamond drew on their and other studies of societal collapses
to formulate his own theory. It follows that the debate in which
Diamond took part was less about the ultimate causes of collapse
and more about which approach better suited the study of human
societies.

Participants in this debate included many of the critics of
Diamond's earlier works. For example, anthropologists writing
on the *Savage Mind* website questioned the soundness of
Diamond's approach to studying human societies, especially its
ethical consequences. They were particularly critical because
they regarded Diamond's approach as the basis of a determinist
argument, even a demonstration of Western superiority.[2]

They identified such environmental determinist logic
in *Guns, Germs, and Steel.*The book argued that European
societies dominated other societies (especially Native Americans,
Indigenous Australians, and Africans) because 13,000 years ago
Europeans were favored by biogeographic factors, such as a milder
climate,* continental axis* (an imaginary line traced horizontally
on a continent whose territory extends for longer from east to
west than from north to south), and a larger number of plants and
animals capable of being domesticated. *Savage Mind* bloggers saw

this approach as based on the assumption that, given a better head start, any society would necessarily develop such fundamentals of all settled states as agriculture and metallurgy earlier than less favored societies. It followed that Diamond's approach was seen to reduce the diverse fates of human societies to the mere influence of the environment.

However, the major consequences of the environmental determinist premise of Diamond's argument were also questioned. In the critics' view, arguing that the environment is the ultimate reason why societies develop in one way or another amounts to an implicit justification for European invasion, domination, and colonialism: in other words, Europeans dominated because they were better served by their environmental conditions; had Native Americans, Indigenous Australians, or Africans been blessed with better environments they would have dominated instead.

The Contemporary Debate

Unconvinced by the criticism, Diamond insisted that environmental and ecological factors have a crucial impact on human history and culture. At the same time, he did not deny that cultural and historical factors and even individual choices play a role in shaping the destiny of human societies. The correct approach, for Diamond, lies somewhere between these two extremes:

- geographic and environmental explanations based on detailed technical facts,
- taking the role of history and culture into account.

The influence of the contemporary debate can be clearly

identified in *Collapse*. In the book, Diamond directly addressed the issue of determinism (the belief that every event has a predetermined cause),[3] reductionism (the explanation of a phenomenon in relation to a relatively small number of factors, and even to a single factor),[4] and of holding societies responsible for their own destiny.[5] Simultaneously, he enriched his methodological toolkit with the ethnographic* methods typically adopted by anthropologists, his most fierce critics. For example, in the first chapter about ecological problems in Montana, he uses ethnography to complement his theory of societal collapse with a wealth of fine-grained details from the everyday life of contemporary Montanans.

Furthermore, he tried to balance his search for synthetic answers with an appreciation of the complications. In this respect, he said: "When I began to plan this book, I didn't appreciate those complications, and I naively thought that the book would just be about environmental damage... I learned that there is no case of a pure environmental collapse."[6] The outcome of Diamond coming to terms with the criticisms is the five-point framework he arrived at in *Collapse*. Rather than a determinist argument that explains the fate of all societies in terms of environmental conditions, this theory takes multiple aspects into consideration. However, that has not necessarily placated his critics.

---

1. Jared M. Diamond, *Guns, Germs, and Steel* (London: Random House, 2013).

2. Kerim Friedman, "From the Archives: Savage Minds vs. Jared Diamond," *Savage Minds*, January 22, 2012, accessed September 30, 2015, http://savageminds.org/2012/01/22/from-the-archives-savage-minds-vs-jared-diamond/.

3. Jared M. Diamond, *Collapse: How Societies Choose to Fail or Survive* (London: Penguin, 2011) 20.

4. Diamond, *Collapse*, 304.

5. Diamond, *Collapse*, 324.

6. Amos Esty, "An Interview with Jared Diamond," *American Scientist Online*, n.d., accessed September 30, 2015, www.americanscientist.org/bookshelf/pub/jared-diamond.

MODULE 4
THE AUTHOR'S CONTRIBUTION

KEY POINTS

* Although Jared Diamond has answered the questions posed in *Collapse* with a well-organized and evidence-based set of answers, whether these answers are satisfactory is a matter of personal judgment.

* Diamond labels his method as "comparative environmental history,"* which consists of comparing in-depth case studies of different societies in order to isolate key variables that provide general explanations.

* *Collapse* does not constitute an innovation in terms of theory, content, or method. Rather, it is innovative in the way it synthesizes an unprecedented quantity of case studies on societal collapse.

Author's Aims

Jared M. Diamond pursued four main objectives in writing *Collapse: How Societies Choose to Fail or Survive.* First, he sought to answer the question of why some civilizations collapse while others solve the problems confronting them and prosper. Second, he attempted to establish similarities between the collapses of different civilizations. Third, he discussed how it is possible to draw lessons for the present from the fate of those societies that survived and those that collapsed. Fourth, and most importantly, he said he wrote *Collapse* to raise awareness of current global environmental problems and to warn against the risks of underestimating the signs of our possible upcoming collapse.

Diamond began with an ethnographic* description of environmental problems in Montana, before moving on to a collection of case studies that illustrate the causes that led a set of selected societies to collapse and others to survive. Past societies are compared with contemporary societies that have either collapsed or undergone crisis management. On the basis of this broad comparison of past and present, collapsed and survived societies, Diamond drew a set of practical lessons for us today.

While Diamond's argument is supported by detailed case studies, some of the studies he quoted (for example, the study of deforestation* in Chaco Canyon in the southwestern United States) have been questioned on the grounds of inaccuracy, which might undermine the solidity of his views. Furthermore, although the book did contribute to making the debate about environmentalism more visible and relevant, it has been argued that Diamond's distinction between "bad" business and businesses that want to protect the environment did a favor to many powerful companies responsible for many of today's environmental problems.[1]

> *"And so what I actually did for 45 years, although it wasn't geography or history, was good unplanned preparation for my present career in geography and history."*
>
> —— Jared Diamond, "About Me," www.jareddiamond.org

Approach

Diamond labels his approach "comparative environmental history," a system that combines methodologies borrowed from biology, geography, and history, and which includes radiocarbon dating* (a method for dating objects through the analysis of radioactive markers), archaeological* and botanical* surveys, and pollen and charcoal analysis* (a method that determines the presence of species of plants in a given territory through the analysis of their remains) and the like. For example, his argument that Easter Island collapsed is supported by analyses of pollen sediments (providing evidence of deforestation) combined with studies of animal bones in garbage dumps (suggesting a decrease in food resources). These analyses are then compared with those conducted in other sites.

He outlined this multidisciplinary* and comparative approach to the study of history in *Natural Experiments of History,* a collection of seven case studies he coedited with the economist and political scientist James Robinson.[*2] The book explains that, although it is not possible to treat societies as if they were bacteria on a Petri dish, comparing in-depth studies of similar societies whose environmental variables differ might provide a general explanation for their fates.

For example, in the southwestern Pacific, the island of Tikopia was able to support a population of 1,200 people for more than 3,000 years thanks to the micromanagement of resources and to birth control. Similarly, Icelanders learned how to avoid soil degradation, enabling them to reach one of the highest per capita incomes* in the world. Though very distant and different, these societies have something in common: they learned how to extract resources from their environment without destroying it.

About the comparative method, Diamond wrote: "I have

belabored this necessity for both good individual studies and good comparisons, because scholars practicing one approach too often belittle the contributions of the other approach... Only from the weight of evidence provided by a comparative study of many societies with different outcomes can one hope to reach convincing conclusions."[3] This approach is not necessarily innovative in anthropology,* although it is less popular than in-depth, long-term ethnography.

Contribution in Context

It is not easy to evaluate *Collapse* as a contribution to a single field. Rather, it contributes to many, including anthropology, archaeology, and history, for it has been questioned by scholars in each of these fields. Diamond does not directly address previous theoretical works on the theme of civilizational collapse (such as those by scholars such as Joseph Tainter*[4] and William M. S. Russell* and Claire Russell*).[5] Instead, he develops an argument on the basis of a comparison of case studies.

In terms of theory building, *Collapse* is an unprecedented synthesis of an unparalleled quantity of case studies of societal collapse. It includes previous analysis of collapsed societies, embraces previous theories of societal collapse, and expands them so as to include the totality of possible combinations of collapse factors. As such, the book makes a considerable contribution to, for example, the anthropologist and historian Joseph Tainter's theory of structural collapse (according to which cultures collapse after reaching an unsustainable degree of complexity, being unable to produce enough organizational and physical energy to support their overdeveloped structure). However, Diamond's theory is not revolutionary to the extent that it draws almost entirely on preexisting material.

With regard to content, *Collapse* is not based on firsthand data; instead it looks to previous in-depth studies. For example, the two chapters about the collapse of the Norse (that is, premodern Scandinavian) colonies overlap partly with the work of Thomas McGovern,* who specializes in climate and island archaeology.[6] To take another example, the equation between the fates of Easter Island and the Earth was advanced by the archaeologist Paul Bahn* and by John Flenley,* an expert in the analysis of ancient particles of dust. So to the extent that *Collapse* does not say much that was not already there, it is not seen as a groundbreaking contribution to the study of societal collapse.

In terms of methodology, Diamond followed the steps of previous comparative studies of societal collapse. For example, Joseph Tainter compared the fate of the Western Roman Empire, the Maya* civilization, and the north American Anasazi* culture, and argued that they collapsed because of a decrease in their social complexity.[7] Diamond agrees with the methodology, but expands it to include and synthesize a larger quantity of case studies. Consequently, he achieves different, more far-reaching conclusions.

---

1. Stephanie McMillan, "The Buying and Selling of Jared Diamond," counterpunch.org, December 12,

2009, accessed September 9, 2015, www.counterpunch.org/2009/12/08/the-buying-and-selling-of-jared-diamond/.

2. Jared M. Diamond and James A. Robinson, eds., *Natural Experiments of History* (Cambridge, MA: Harvard University Press, 2010).

3. Jared M. Diamond, *Collapse: How Societies Choose to Fail or Survive* (London: Penguin, 2011), 17.

4. Joseph Tainter, *The Collapse of Complex Societies* (Cambridge: Cambridge University Press, 1988).

5. Claire Russell and William M. S. Russell, "Population Crises and Population Cycles," *Medicine, Conflict and Survival* 16, no. 4 (2000): 383–410.

6. Thomas McGovern et al., "Northern Islands, Human Error, and Environmental Degradation: A View of Social and Ecological Change in the Medieval North Atlantic," *Human Ecology* 16 (1988).

7. Tainter, Collapse of Complex Societies.

SECTION 2
IDEAS

MAIN IDEAS

KEY POINTS

* Jared M. Diamond says a combination of five key factors causes human civilizations to collapse. The most important is the fifth: a society's ability to respond to the other four factors.

* Diamond takes examples from past societies to illustrate why some succumbed because of the five factors, and why some were able to survive their crises.

* Diamond finds a balance between a scientific and accessible language with a storytelling approach to scientific writing that captures readers as it informs them.

Key Themes

In *Collapse: How Societies Choose to Fail or Survive*, Jared M. Diamond suggests that a combination of five key factors causes human civilizations to collapse. The first factor is environmental degradation,* including deforestation,* pollution, soil depletion, erosion* (the movement of soil and rock from one place to another as a result of rain, wind, agriculture, and deforestation) and overpopulation. The extent of such degradation depends on two environmental subfactors: fragility (susceptibility to damage) and resilience* (potential for recovery). These subfactors, in turn, depend on people—who cut trees, for example, or catch fish at sustainable* or unsustainable rates— and the environment itself, which is either more or less capable of sustaining human action.

The second factor is climate change,* which has historically been natural but is today caused by human action, and consists of long-term and large-scale variations in rainfall, temperature, humidity, and the like. Hotter, colder, wetter, drier, or more or less variable climates cause drought, unbearable temperatures, reduced crop yields, and food shortages. For example, a severe drought hit the Maya,* in the area that today is Mexico, Guatemala, Belize, the western part of El Salvador, and Honduras, and the Anasazi* of the American Southwest; similarly, the Norse ("Viking") colonies in Greenland were unable to survive the Little Ice Age*—a cold period of climatic history between about 1400 and 1800.

The third factor is increased hostility by neighboring groups. Indeed, "collapses for ecological or other reasons often masquerade as military defeats."[1]

The fourth is the reverse of the third, the withdrawal of support and trade from friendly neighbors. Indeed, most societies "depend to some extent on friendly neighbors... for imports of essential trade goods."[2]

The fifth factor is a society's ability to respond to its problems. While the four factors above may or may not prove significant for a particular collapse, the fifth factor has always and everywhere proved crucial.

The key lesson is, therefore, that even if societies perceive their problems, they are not necessarily able to solve them. Whether a society is able to counter any of the above factors, or a combination of the four, largely depends on its cultural values and its political, economic, and social institutions.

"For the first time in history, we face the risk of a global decline. But we also are the first to enjoy the opportunity of learning quickly from developments in societies anywhere else in the world today, and from what has unfolded in societies at any time in the past. That's why I wrote this book."

— Jared M. Diamond, *Collapse: How Societies Choose to Fail or Survive*

Exploring the Ideas

Diamond takes examples from past societies to illustrate why some succumbed because of the five factors and some were able to survive.

Easter Island in the southeast Pacific is an example of collapse caused by the first factor. Society there fell because all of the palm trees were chopped down to make canoes and rollers to transport their *moai:* the giant statues dotted around the island. The people did not know that this particular type of palm would not recover as fast as the palms of other Polynesian islands. In addition, the island chiefs competed for self-promotion and pushed the logging activity to the point of no return. As a consequence, the island fauna (animals) died out, the agricultural system soon proved insufficient to feed the entire population, and they eventually turned to internal warfare and cannibalism. Easter Island, Diamond concludes, "is as close as we can get to a 'pure' ecological collapse, in this case due to total deforestation."[3]

The Norse colonies of Greenland, to take a different example, collapsed as a result of all five factors—but especially because the

Scandinavian colonists were unable to change their values and take corrective action. For them, "it was out of the question to invest less in churches, to imitate or intermarry with the Inuit, and thereby to face an eternity in Hell just in order to survive another winter on Earth."[4] Ultimately, it is such a rigidity of values that caused their collapse.

In contrast, three examples of societies that overcame deforestation, erosion, and soil infertility illustrate the importance of flexibility and corrective action.

At the beginning of seventeenth century, the Tokugawa* shoguns of Japan—the ruling elite—tackled deforestation with the imposition of resource management policies even though that meant less wood was available for their spectacular palaces. And the Highlanders of Papua New Guinea used their botanical* knowledge—their study of plants—to increase soil fertility and reforestation* when a wood crisis followed the growth of the farming population about 7,000 years ago.

The chiefs of the island of Tikopia, apart from their regular micromanagement of food production, took the bitter decision at some point in 1600 C.E. to exterminate their highly valued pigs because they were destroying their crops. This action was taken even though, as Diamond writes, "pigs are the sole large domestic animal and a principal status symbol of Melanesian societies."[5] Unlike their Easter Island counterparts, these chiefs valued their survival more than their status.

Language and Expression

The main stylistic challenge in *Collapse,* as in other books by

Diamond, is finding the right balance between scientific and accessible language. In order to support his conclusions, Diamond has to include a wealth of technical details borrowed from the fields of geography, anthropology,* archaeology,* and botany. He is aware that the average layperson and even the student might lack the necessary knowledge to keep all these details in mind and, simultaneously, follow the overall argument. Thus, Diamond balances the amount of technicalities with a series of anecdotes that exemplify a point.

For example, as an illustration of the fifth factor, he writes,"What did the Easter Islander who cut the last palm tree say while he was doing it?"[6] To express the concept of resource management, he tells us, "As my Norwegian archaeologist friend Christian Keller expressed it, 'Life in Greenland is all about finding the good patches of useful resources.'"[7] Here, the "Malthusian trap"* is important; this is the English economist Thomas Malthus's theory that the exponential growth of human beings tends to surpass food production. Referencing this idea, Diamond discusses the Rwandan* genocide (in the course of which some 500,000–1,000,000 people, largely of the Tutsi ethnic group, were murdered by members of the Hutu ethnic group), noting, "Friends of mine who visited Rwanda in 1984 sensed an ecological disaster in the making."[8]

The repeated use of "friends" from distant places has at least three major outcomes. First, it puts "a personal face on a subject that could otherwise seem abstract."[9] Second, it makes the reader feel much closer to issues that would otherwise feel foreign, distant, and perhaps even irrelevant. Third, it presents the search for scientific knowledge more like a worldwide conversation among "friends," rather than a painstaking debate between nitpicking specialists gathered in an ivory tower.

In this way, he creates a sort of scientific storytelling that captures readers at the same time as it educates them.

---

1. Jared M. Diamond, *Collapse: How Societies Choose to Fail or Survive* (London: Penguin, 2011), 11.
2. Diamond, *Collapse*, 12.
3. Diamond, *Collapse*, 18.
4. Diamond, *Collapse*, 247.
5. Diamond, *Collapse*, 521.
6. Diamond, *Collapse*, 112.
7. Diamond, *Collapse*, 210.
8. Diamond, *Collapse*, 318.
9. Diamond, *Collapse*, 30.

SECONDARY IDEAS

KEY POINTS

- Although contemporary global societies are threatened by the same kind of factors that destroyed past civilizations, they are in a better position to face these challenges.

- Diamond takes examples from contemporary and past societies to illustrate that they face similar challenges, and to draw lessons on how to avoid the risk of collapse.

- Even though past societies were deeply damaged by five key factors associated with social collapse, some did not disappear entirely. While Diamond did not explore this resilience, he looked at why some societies survived.

Other Ideas

After establishing the main factors causing societies to fail, in *Collapse: How Societies Choose to Fail or Survive*, Jared M. Diamond seeks to demonstrate that it is possible to draw parallels between past and present societies. These parallels suggest that as long as societies are subject to the same processes, they also share the same fates. The result is that they allow us to predict the collapse of contemporary global societies.

Present and past societies share many problems of environmental degradation* (Diamond's first factor): "The processes through which past societies have undermined themselves by damaging their environments fall into eight categories, whose relative importance differs from case to case: deforestation* and habitat destruction; soil problems (erosion,* salinization,* and soil fertility losses); water management* problems; overhunting; overfishing; the impact of introduced species on native species; human population growth; and the increased human impact as disposable incomes rise."[1]

Further, Diamond highlights important differences, which encourage us to consider innovative solutions to avoid the collapse of contemporary global societies. "The environmental problems facing us today include the same eight that undermined past societies, plus four new ones: human-caused climate change,* buildup of toxic chemicals in the environment, energy shortages, and full human utilization of the Earth's photosynthetic capacity."*[2] Globalization*—the increasing convergence of political, economic, and social ties across continents—is responsible for the four additional problems.

Globalization is also part of the solution, however: "We also are the first to enjoy the opportunity of learning quickly from developments in societies anywhere else in the world today, and from what has unfolded in societies at any time in the past."[3] Here Diamond is implicitly saying that his writing the book is itself an example of the kind of capacity for reflection on the past that distinguishes modern society from that of the Easter Islanders, for instance.

> *"But there are also differences between the modern world and its problems, and those past societies and their problems. We shouldn't be so naïve as to think that study of the past will yield simple solutions, directly transferable to our societies today."*
>
> ——Jared M. Diamond, *Collapse: How Societies Choose to Fail or Survive*

Exploring the Ideas

Diamond argues that the problems faced by societies in the past and those faced by contemporary societies can be generally grouped into the same categories: the five key factors.

For example, the Norse ("Vikings") exhausted their irreplaceable resources of turf to build houses and to burn as fuel. This played an important part in their collapse. Similarly, the United States, China, and other contemporary societies are currently consuming an unsustainable quantity of fuel. Fuel exhaustion will arguably cause, at least in part, the collapse of societies unable to find alternative sources of energy.

To take another example, Easter Islanders pursued the increase in their chiefdoms'* status by building large statues at the expense of their forests. Similarly, industrialized societies seem unable to refrain from increasing their rates of production, even though they live on a planet with finite resources. Easter Islanders could not rely on trade partners. Similarly, inhabitants of Earth cannot seek the support of other planets. Hence, we should value our resources higher than our production.

We can look to the past for solutions to the problems faced by contemporary societies; the Japanese shoguns of the Tokugawa* period (1603–1868) avoided a self-inflicted deforestation thanks to their awareness of the risks and their willingness to impose measures to manage their forests. Similarly, thanks to the imposition of environmental policies by two dictators, Rafael Trujillo* and Joaquin Balaguer,* the Dominican Republic avoided the environmental degradation experienced throughout the nineteenth and twentieth centuries by its neighbor Haiti.

Whether we will be able to avoid our own collapse largely depends on our capacity to tackle the 12 environmental problems identified by Diamond. Further, he argues that it is possible to recognize signs both of hope and of despair; he says some modern businesses "are among the most environmentally destructive forces today, while others provide some of the most effective environmental protection."[4] As in the past, these powerful players might choose to pursue their own goals at the expense of society or at sustainable rates.

Overlooked

One aspect that has been overlooked in *Collapse* is Diamond's acknowledgment that collapse and survival often coexist. In the book, he generally places more emphasis on the collapse of societies rather than the survival of their vestiges or people. This is perhaps unsurprising, and legitimate, given that his is a book about collapse rather than survival or resilience. However, Diamond did recognize that some people survived the collapse of their societies. For example, he noted that the extinct North American Anasazi* people did not entirely vanish and that their descendants currently inhabit contemporary Native American societies.[5]

Diamond's recognition that a degree of resilience is present in collapsed societies has not been given much academic credence. For example, the anthropologists Patricia McAnany* and Norman Yoffee* argued that Diamond's failure to recognize that no society simply disappears severely undermines his argument.[6] It is true that Diamond dealt only with the descendants of the Anasazi and other collapsed societies briefly and did not further analyze their persistence—but it is important, however, that he has at least mentioned their survival, as this balances a view of collapse as extreme population decline and loss of culture with an image of endurance and adaptation.

McAnany and Yoffee criticized Diamond for underestimating societal resilience. For example, to oppose his argument about the collapse of the Maya Empire, they argued that even though some Maya cities were dramatically depopulated in the eighth and ninth centuries, the population of other regions of the Mayan Empire simultaneously increased. Furthermore, people of Maya descent lived in the populous cities of the postclassic period* of the region's history (about 950–1539), and seven million people currently inhabit contemporary Mexico and northern Central America.

If adequately combined, the concept of collapse and resilience would potentially grant a much deeper theoretical understanding of human societies. It might be argued, for instance, that collapses are processes of destructive creation in which societies undergo a redefinition of their relationship with the environment through the development of a new culture.

1. Jared M. Diamond, *Collapse: How Societies Choose to Fail or Survive* (London: Penguin, 2011), 4.

2. Diamond, *Collapse*, 5.

3. Diamond, *Collapse*, 11.

4. Diamond, *Collapse*, 11.

5. Diamond, *Collapse*, 135.

6. Patricia A. McAnany and Norman Yoffee, eds., *Questioning Collapse: Human Resilience, Ecological Vulnerability, and the Aftermath of Empire* (New York: Cambridge University Press, 2010).

MODULE 7
ACHIEVEMENT

KEY POINTS

- While Diamond's argument in *Collapse* is not necessarily revolutionary, the book has a number of merits, for which it has been praised.

- *Collapse*'s most important achievement is to provide an evidence-based argument in support of an already widespread, if controversial, opinion: saving our planet depends on managing the environment.

- Although a best seller, *Collapse* was less successful than Diamond's earlier work *Guns, Germs, and Steel*—possibly because he was attempting to incorporate too much, resulting in a longer, less readable book.

Assessing the Argument

In *Collapse: How Societies Choose to Fail or Survive*, Jared M. Diamond achieved his stated aim. He established a general theory of societal collapse on the basis of comparisons between numerous case studies of both past and present societies, concluding that five key factors cause the fall of these societies. But although his argument is solid and well demonstrated, it did not necessarily challenge previous understandings of societal collapse.

Listing the five key collapse factors, Diamond merely reorganizes and confirms previous conclusions, expanding them on the basis of a broader comparison of cases. Similarly, it is also apparent that the crucial collapse factor—a society's capacity to take corrective action—may be considered self-evident, even if the point had a considerable impact on the environmental debate.[1]

It follows that Diamond strongly emphasizes the environment as the main cause of societal collapse (while acknowledging other factors such as relations with neighboring groups). Yet, equally, a society's ability to respond to its decline depends above all on its values—its culture, in other words. Diamond insists that this is the most important factor likely to save a society from collapse. Thus it appears that Diamond places equal importance on environment and culture alike.

> If I had the power and means to change only one thing of the world today, that one thing would be my being limited to change only one thing in the world today: my one change would be to give myself the power to make many changes. That's because, as I discuss in the last chapter of Collapse, we face a dozen different major problems, all of which we must succeed in solving, and any one of which alone could do us in even if we solved the other eleven."
>
> ——Penguin Reader's Guide, "A Conversation with Jared Diamond"

Achievement in Context

In writing *Collapse*, Diamond did not draw heavily on firsthand ("primary") research. For the most part, he includes personal experiences only in order to provide readers with informal anecdotes that make his analysis more accessible. His fundamental argument is mainly supported by previous historical, anthropological,* archaeological,* and environmental studies, which Diamond distills to form a self-contained answer to his question.

In so doing, he undeniably performs an important service to the study of societal collapse. Indeed, he demonstrates that identifying threads that could be interwoven from so many diverse studies is anything but simple.

The current importance of the environmental debate and the political implications of Diamond's conclusions can also explain the success of his book. He argues that the crucial factor in a societal collapse is the ability of a society, especially of its leaders, to reverse decline. Exactly as was the case in Tikopia in the Pacific, in Japan of the Tokugawa* period (1603–1868), or in the modern Dominican Republic, contemporary leaders can change the destiny of their societies by imposing certain policies.

The wide success of *Collapse* is also due to Diamond's second book, *Guns, Germs, and Steel*,[2] which was awarded several prizes, translated into 25 languages, and sold more than a million copies. People who loved the book's sweeping comparisons about cultures were eager to read another mammoth synthesis of the world's failures and successes—as indeed were those who disagreed with it.

However, like *Guns, Germs, and Steel*, *Collapse* was much more widely appreciated by the general public than by specialists. The latter claimed that the book was flawed, biased, and plainly wrong in many aspects. In contrast, the general public was not necessarily interested in the ideology behind the book or what were asserted to be its scholarly imprecisions. Rather, what non-specialists found valuable was a clear and well-argued case for a conclusion in support of an already widespread opinion: if we want to save our planet, we have to take wise steps to manage the environment. That, perhaps, is the most important achievement of *Collapse.*

Limitations

Diamond argued that the fifth factor—a society's ability to take corrective actions to stave off its own collapse—is the most important factor in a society's survival, this being the single factor that he identified in all the analyzed cases of societal collapse. That said, Diamond does not really explain what this factor comprises.

It is clear that, according to Diamond, the fifteenth-century Norse settlers of Greenland collapsed because they were unable to change their values and learn from the indigenous Inuit people how to cope better with their environment. Similarly, it seems logical that Easter Islanders should have initiated a cultural change at some point between the fifteenth and the seventeenth centuries so as not to cut down their entire forests for the purposes of transporting statues and making canoes. Diamond does not, however, explain what it means to change a culture.

Diamond is much more effective when he describes societies that avoided their collapse; for instance, thanks to the imposition of policies of tree management on the part of the Japanese shoguns or bottom-up micromanagement of horticultural gardens in the Highlands of Papua New Guinea. In other words, it is not difficult to imagine these individual decisions implemented for a higher benefit. What is not clear, however, is how these individual decisions can be considered as an expression of the culture of a people, rather than a set of decisions dictated by the emerging circumstances.

On the basis of the kind of sweeping comparisons upon which so much of Diamond's work is based, it might be possible to isolate a definition of culture as a system of values that can be modified depending on the circumstances. And indeed Diamond does imply, if nothing more, such a concept on the basis of his cross-cultural comparisons. Nonetheless, it remains the case that, while culture occupies the central role in Diamond's theory, it is a concept only partially defined in *Collapse*.

---

1. William Rees, "Contemplating the Abyss," *Nature* 433, no. 7021 (2005): 15–16.
2. Donald Kennedy, "The Choice: Finding Hope in the History of Environmental Ruin," *Foreign Affairs* 84, no. 2 (2005): 134.

MODULE 8
PLACE IN THE AUTHOR'S WORK

KEY POINTS

* Diamond published *Collapse* after achieving worldwide renown with his work *Guns, Germs, and Steel*. Unsurprisingly, the two books have much in common, including style, methodology, and the main question of their research.

* *Collapse* is an integration of many aspects of Diamond's life, including his career, his personal experiences, and his relationships with his public, his coworkers, his friends, and even his enemies.

* While *Collapse* is not the most successful of Jared Diamond's books, it illustrates his life journey as a scholar who began with hard sciences* and then turned to social sciences and popular science writing.

Positioning

Jared M. Diamond was already a world-famous scholar when *Collapse: How Societies Choose to Fail or Survive* was published in 2005. He had come to the attention of the general public with *The Third Chimpanzee*,[1] which won the 1992 Rhône-Poulenc Prize for Science Books and the *Los Angeles Times* Book Prize.

His second book, *Guns, Germs, and Steel*,[2] received worldwide acclaim and several awards, including the Pulitzer Prize in 1998, an Aventis Prize for Science Books, and the 1997 Phi Beta Kappa Award in Science. It was in 1997 that his career really reached a peak. The popular *Why Is Sex Fun?* was also published in that year.

Later, Diamond spent more than five years researching and analyzing the material to write *Collapse.* He was already experienced in drawing together, for the purposes of comparison, substantial quantities of material, covering the entire globe and time spans as long as 13,000 years.

In *Guns, Germs, and Steel*, he used the comparative method* to ask and answer the question of why Europeans were able to dominate the indigenous peoples of Australia, Africa, and the Americas rather than the other way around. His response was a list of environmental causes followed by a series of feedback loops (self-perpetuating cycles of improvements). With *Collapse*, he used the same comparative method, this time to answer another, if related, question: why do societies collapse? The answer, again, is a list of environmental factors that caused some societies to be more favored and others to be less favored.

Although Diamond did not conceive of *Collapse* as a companion to *Guns, Germs, and Steel*, there is a clear intellectual connection between the two books.

> *"Diamond is probably the best-known writer of anthropology even though he is not an anthropologist! "*
>
> —— Patricia A. McAnany and Norman Yoffee,
> *Questioning Collapse*

Integration

Diamond's intellectual life has had an undeniable influence on his publications. When he was a young PhD student in the field of physiology,* he began by publishing in the specialist field of gall bladder studies. Later, he tried to communicate his interests in physiology with a book unashamedly aimed at general readers, *The Third Chimpanzee.*

At the same time, thanks to his parallel interest in ornithology,* he was increasingly comparing different populations of birds. In the 1990s, working on *Guns, Germs, and Steel*, he combined his ability to write for the general public, his interest in the comparative method, and his recent fascination with human history. The result was his coronation as one of the most important scientists of the decade.

The reaction of the academic world to *Guns, Germs, and Steel* was not, however, always positive. Diamond took academic criticism very seriously; in *Collapse* he made an explicit attempt to avoid charges of ethnocentrism* (tending to adopt one's own cultural theories and values to examine and evaluate other peoples' cultures), social Darwinism* (the discredited idea that individuals and societies are subject to the same evolutionary pressures as biological species), and environmental determinism* (the theory that the environment determines the historical paths of a society associated with a particular territory).

For example, he praises non-Western societies such as the shoguns of Tokugawa-era* Japan, the Polynesians of Tikopia, and the Highlanders of Papua New Guinea for their skillful management of their environmental resources.That seems to have been done in order to avoid charges of ethnocentrism.To take another example, the first chapter of *Collapse* looks more like an ethnography*—a study of the customs, habits, and beliefs of a people—rather than a sweeping comparison.

The book, as a result, includes more ethnography, technical passages, and specific references to academic debates than *Guns, Germs, and Steel*. Diamond also alludes to his anti-racism more frequently in *Collapse* than in *Guns, Germs, and Steel*, as if repetition could clarify a point that he thought he had made already. All this seems to be done to avoid the attacks of his critics.

Significance

Although *Collapse* is not the most successful of Diamond's books, it illustrates his journey as a scholar who began in the so-called hard sciences before turning to social sciences to address what he considered critical questions concerning humanity. To this end, he adopted an approach he called "comparative environmental history"* (a term he uses to describe the study of human societies by comparing in-depth case studies in order to isolate key variables that provide general explanations), writing plain and accessible English to reach the widest possible public.

While Diamond received public acclaim as a result, he was widely attacked by specialists. That had the effect of balancing his intellectual wit with a dose of theoretical humility.[3] In turn, he showed social scientists the power of using "comparative environmental history" in a radically critical way.

Despite the fact that both sides of the controversy appear to have gained something, this does not mean that the debate between Diamond and his academic critics has been resolved. Diamond is constantly charged with being a defender of earlier Western imperialism* and a champion of geographic determinism*.

Paradoxically, *Collapse* and *Guns, Germs, and Steel* make plain that, for Diamond, the successes and failures of civilizations do not depend on racial superiority. Rather, in Diamond's view, societies are more or less inclined to develop and collapse as a result of their environmental circumstances. At the same time, collapse and recovery are also the result of other factors, including chance, which demonstrate the multicausative* nature of Diamond's theory as opposed to the determinist position his critics attribute to him ("multicausative" indicates, simply, that a fact results from many causes). Whatever the criticisms of him, then, both books make robust cases.

The significance of Diamond's work is also his message that history and science are not necessarily specialist fields for an intellectual elite. When he explains how he conceived of *Collapse*, it would seem as though anyone sufficiently interested and disciplined might have written it: "It's simple. It was the most fascinating as well as the most important subject I could think of, and one that I'd been interested in for decades, just as many people develop a romantic interest in sites of collapsed societies, like the Maya cities overgrown by jungle or the Anasazi* skyscrapers in the US desert. So there was this romantic mystery that drew me to it."[4]

It follows that one merit of *Collapse* is in making the public feel that science and history can be fun; as such it provides an accessible way to make up your mind on some deeply fascinating questions about humankind.

1. Jared M. Diamond, *The Third Chimpanzee: The Evolution and Future of the Human Animal* (London: HarperCollins, 2006).
2. Jared M. Diamond, *Guns, Germs, and Steel* (London: Random House, 2013).
3. See, for example: John R. McNeill, "A Usable Past," *American Scientist* 93, no. 2 (2005): 172–5.
4. Amos Esty, "An Interview with Jared Diamond," *American Scientist Online*, n.d., accessed September 30, 2015, www.americanscientist.org/bookshelf/pub/jared-diamond.

SECTION 3
IMPACT

THE FIRST RESPONSES

KEY POINTS

* *Collapse* was praised for making a firm point, accessible to a wide audience, in the environmental debate. But it was also severely criticized for the methodology and its alleged ideological premises.

* Although in *Collapse* Diamond had already written "preventive responses" to his critics, the book received those anticipated critiques anyway. Diamond published his responses in relevant journals.

* Sometimes the debate has taken a bitter tone—perhaps on account of what the book represents, politically, ideologically, and morally, in the eyes of the critics, rather than what it says.

Criticism

Jared M. Diamond's *Collapse: How Societies Choose to Fail or Survive* became a best seller in the United States a few days after its publication, perhaps in the wake of the success of *Guns, Germs, and Steel*.[1] It received widespread praise in important newspapers and magazines around the world. In general, favorable reviewers of *Collapse* welcomed the argument advanced by Diamond and its practical impact on society.

For example, William Rees,* a scholar of climate* and sustainable development, noted that *Collapse* makes a firm point in an environmental debate dominated by uncertainty and lack of consensus.[2] Rees praises Diamond for demonstrating that, throughout human history, the crucial variable in the environmental destiny of societies has been the responsibility of people and particularly of their leaders.

Diamond has also been praised for his ability to engage readers from different disciplines or who don't have previous knowledge in any of the specific subjects.[3] In fact, even his critics admit that academic specialization "creates distance from interested laypersons and inquisitive students."[4]

Critics, however, attacked *Collapse* both for the methodology used to support the argument and for its alleged ideological starting points. It is possible to classify these negative reactions into four major themes.

First, critics argued that *Collapse* "represents the persistence of an environmental determinist logic... referred to as neo-environmental determinism."*[5] That is, they insist that Diamond explains the successes and failures of human societies as mere products of environmental conditions.

Second, critics insisted that Diamond's environmental determinism justifies Western imperialism* (roughly, the ideology justifying the rule of European powers over large territories in Africa, Oceania, and the Americas). The anthropologist Frederick K. Errington* aptly summarized the point: "The haves prosper because of happenstance beyond their control, while the have-nots are responsible for their own demise."[6]

Third, by failing to recognize that no society disappears entirely, this would appear to compromise the validity of the term "collapse"; it is possible, for example, to identify descendants of the Maya, the Indians of the American Southwest, and so on. This point has been particularly stressed by the contributors to the volume *Questioning Collapse*, a work published with the explicit aim of criticizing Diamond's book.[7]

Fourth, Diamond has been accused of ignoring some facts. For example, the archaeologist and anthropologist Terry Hunt* and the archaeologist Carl Lipo* argued that the deforestation* of Easter Island was caused by predatory Polynesian rats, not by the islanders, whose population remained stable until the Europeans brought diseases and slavery[8]—a thesis also put forward by the anthropologist Benny Peiser.*[9]

> "For Wilcox*, the notion that the great architectural achievements of the Chaco Canyon can be labeled a societal failure constitutes an example of 'reverse engineering,' meaning the assignation of past failure to contemporary people who have been economically and politically disenfranchised as a direct result of colonial expansion and a European-derived population."
>
> —— Patricia McAnany and Norman Yoffee,
> *Questioning Collapse*

Responses

In a sense, there was no need to answer the charge of environmental determinism. In *Collapse*, Diamond had already made clear that his argument was not simply a matter of determinism but depended on many explanations; as one scholar has put it, "environmental deterioration always operates as a force among other forces."[10]

However, Diamond responded to this and other criticisms on multiple occasions.

He asserted that his critics are biased by the implicit assumption that all geographical explanations are necessarily racist. For him, they are still blindly reacting to the racist tendencies in the social sciences of the nineteenth and twentieth centuries.[11]

Concerning the charge of cultural imperialism, Diamond says he does not blame collapsed societies for their own collapses but rather praises those individuals and groups who take corrective action. For example, the case of preventative polices enacted in the Dominican Republic illustrates that "leaders who don't just react passively, who have the courage to anticipate crises or to act early, and who make strong insightful decisions of top-down management really can make a huge difference to their societies."[12]

With regard to the definition of collapse, for Diamond it "makes no sense to redefine as heartwarmingly resilient a society in which everyone ends up dead, or in which most of the population vanishes, or that loses writing, state government and great art for centuries."[13] Diamond thinks that only those who do not have the necessary knowledge of animals, plants, soils, and climates can deny the destruction that results from environmental degradation.*[14]

In terms of the historical facts, Diamond notes that deforestation in Easter Island cannot be attributed to rats, which were present in other Polynesian islands without necessarily causing deforestation. He adds that this and other conclusions by Hunt and Lipo "are considered transparently wrong by essentially all other archaeologists with active programs on Easter Island."[15]

Conflict and Consensus

Whether some consensus is found between Diamond and his critics largely depends on the tone of the debate and the content of the criticism. For example, Diamond writes, "whenever I hear the words 'geographic determinism,' I know that I am about to hear a reflex dismissal of geographic considerations, an opinion not worth listening to or reading, and an excuse for intellectual laziness and for not coming to grips with real issues." In contrast, when a journalist asked Diamond whether any criticism caused him to rethink aspects of the book, he responded, "Details, yes; main thrusts of my argument, no."[16] It follows that some critics were rightly pointing at certain inaccuracies, whereas others have been dismissed for failing to provide evidence to back up their criticisms.

In general, however, the distance between Diamond and his critics means that agreement is always unlikely. Rather, arguments tend to be dismissed on the grounds of incompetence and lack of specialist knowledge. If Diamond says that his critics are not trained geographers,[17] for example, they respond by asserting that he is not a trained historian.[18] It is not always productive.

The fact that neither side is able to engage on equal terms is not to be understood as a consequence of what Diamond actually says in *Collapse*, which is mostly a synthesis of arguments advanced by previous scholars. Rather, the reasons behind the vitriolic tone of Diamond's critics stem more from what they hold the book to represent politically, ideologically, and morally—perhaps their true objection.

1. Donald Kennedy, "The Choice: Finding Hope in the History of Environmental Ruin," *Foreign Affairs* 84, no. 2 (2005): 134–8.

2. William Rees, "Contemplating the Abyss," *Nature* 433, no. 7021 (January 6, 2005): 15–16.

3. John R. McNeill, "A Usable Past," *American Scientist* 93, no. 2 (March 1, 2005): 174.

4. Patricia A. McAnany and Norman Yoffee, eds., *Questioning Collapse: Human Resilience, Ecological Vulnerability, and the Aftermath of Empire* (New York, NY: Cambridge University Press, 2010), 4.

5. Gabriel Judkins et al., "Determinism within Human—Environment Research and the Rediscovery of Environmental Causation," *The Geographical Journal* 174, no. 1 (2008): 18.

6. George Johnson, "A Question of Blame When Societies Fall," *The New York Times*, December 25, 2007, accessed September 30, 2015, www.nytimes. com/2007/12/25/science/25diam.html.

7. McAnany and Yoffee, *Questioning Collapse.*

8. Terry Hunt and Carl Lipo, "Ecological Catastrophe, Collapse, and the Myth of 'Ecocide' on Rapa Nui (Easter Island)," in *Questioning Collapse,* McAnany and Yoffee, 223–46.

9. Benny Peiser, "From Genocide to Ecocide: The Rape of Rapa Nui," *Energy & Environment* 16, no. 3 (2005): 513–40.

10. McNeill, "A Usable Past," 172.

11. Jared M. Diamond, "Geographic Determinism: What Does 'Geographic Determinism' Really Mean?," jareddiamond.org, n.d., accessed September 30, 2015, www.jareddiamond.org/Jared_Diamond/Geographic_determinism.html.

12. Jared M. Diamond, *Collapse: How Societies Choose to Fail or Survive* (London: Penguin, 2011), 304.

13. Jared M. Diamond, "Two Views of Collapse," *Nature* 463, no. 7283 (2010): 881.

14. Diamond, "Geographic Determinism."

15. Mark Lynas, "The Myths of Easter Island—Jared Diamond Responds," marklynas.org, September 22, 2011, accessed September 10, 2015, www.marklynas.org/2011/09/the-myths-of-easter-island-jared-diamond-responds/.

16. Penguin Reader's Guide, "A Conversation with Jared Diamond," penguin. com, n.d., accessed September 9, 2015, www.penguin.com/read/book-clubs/collapse/9780143117001.

17. Diamond, "Geographic Determinism."

18. Anthony J. McMichael, "Collapse. How Societies Choose to Fail or Succeed. Jared Diamond," *International Journal of Epidemiology* 35, no. 2 (April 1, 2006): 499–500.

THE EVOLVING DEBATE

KEY POINTS

- It could be argued that in the academic debate about indigenous rights and Western imperialism,* Diamond's arguments have been misrepresented.

- Much of the debate between Diamond and his opponents has been dominated by the projection of different approaches to knowledge concerning the degree to which comparisons are useful or possible.

- In current scholarship, debates about factual evidence and methodology tend simply to stall in the face of an apparently implacable hostility between Diamond and many anthropologists.

Uses and Problems

In an academic context, the problem with using the theory proposed by Jared M. Diamond's *Collapse: How Societies Choose to Fail or Survive* is that the debate over its value is not necessarily about what the work argues but, rather, about what its critics claim it argues. For example, in the article "F**k Jared Diamond," the American scholar and activist David Correia* writes, "Everything Diamond does is motivated by an environmental determinism* that takes the physical environment, including the climate,* to be a determinant on human society."[1] As Diamond explains, however, "in the strict sense [environmental determinism] is not a view that any sensible person espouses today. Instead, historians who discuss environmental influences on history at all are often caricatured by critics as 'environmental determinists,' supposedly meaning someone who believes that the environment strictly determines human history and that human choices count for nothing."[2] It seems that *Collapse*, like *Guns, Germs, and Steel*, is held to be a product of this old school of environmental determinist thought without the book necessarily espousing this school's tenets.

Hence, the charge of determinism is not necessarily associated with the book's argument. Instead, the ferocity of the debate is perhaps better explained by preexisting tensions between Diamond and his critics. For example, some anthropologists have criticized Diamond because his theory allegedly supports the "ideology of an imperial capitalism," as the geographer Dick Peet* called it[3] (capitalism being the economic and social system, dominant in the West today, in which trade and industry are held in private hands). In contrast, some anthropologists see themselves as defenders of indigenous rights against what they consider the homogenizing forces of globalization* (the convergence of political, economic, and cultural ties and habits across continents) and the socioeconomic inequalities introduced by Western capitalism.[4] Neither view is necessarily valid, for Diamond never explicitly justified Western imperialism, and no indigenous people see themselves as requiring the kind of protection that some anthropologists extend to them. But there is a case to be made that in the course of the debate, Diamond has been attacked for views he does not hold.

> *"In offering this framework, Diamond goes beyond simplistic formulations about ecological collapse, recognizing that environmental deterioration always operates as a force among other forces, and sometimes in synergistic conjunction with other forces."*
>
> ——John R. McNeill, "A Usable Past"

Schools of Thought

Another interpretation concerns the ways in which *Collapse* was used in the debate about the opposition between nomothetic* and ideographic approaches.* "Nomothetic" describes the possibility of deriving general ideas or laws from a set of particular facts; "ideographic," by contrast, describes the assumption that no phenomena are truly comparable, and only concrete properties are worthy of description.

Although an argument of very long standing, the fact that the controversy was still alive at the time when Diamond was forming his ideas is evidenced by a debate in 1988 at the University of Manchester; on that occasion, 37 anthropologists voted against the motion that their discipline was a generalizing science while 26 agreed with it.

Almost three decades later, the anthropologist Alex Golub* wrote that "the one lesson [American] anthropologists want to spread across the world is 'It's complicated.' In classrooms and publications, our goal is to show the complexity of human life to our audiences. To the horror of nomothetic, model-making sciences, for us 'abstraction' and 'simplification' are often pejorative terms."[5] This shows that the opposition is still alive today.

In *Collapse*, Diamond's intention was not necessarily to persuade his critics that cross-cultural comparison and the natural experiment* are infallible scientific methods. However, the skepticism with which anthropologists read *Collapse* relates to a more general dissatisfaction with all-encompassing arguments about human societies as opposed to those emphasizing complexity.

This emphasis on complexity dates back at least to the days of the pioneering anthropologist Franz Boas,* who strongly rejected the possibility of establishing general theories about all human societies. He insisted that the goal of anthropology was ethnographic* description, based on what he called "historical particularism" (roughly, the idea that any society is the product of its unique historical circumstances). Other anthropologists have nevertheless attempted to establish general theories. For example, it is on the basis of cross-cultural comparisons that in 1925 the influential French sociologist Marcel Mauss* wrote *The Gift*, perhaps the most popular book in anthropology.

It follows that the opposition between nomothetic and idiographic approaches is inherent to anthropology itself rather than one which sets up anthropologists in opposition to Diamond.

In Current Scholarship

Arguably, the widespread popularity and success of Diamond's work has, to specialists, been detrimental to the diffusion of the points he has made. Indeed, his arguments have repeatedly been appropriated and misrepresented. It is a distortion of his views common to both the academic and the wider world.

In a speech in Jerusalem in 2012, the conservative US politician Mitt Romney* referred to Diamond's work to support his view that the differences between Israel and Palestine in terms of industrial development could be explained as the consequences of cultural differences. That was fundamental to his contention that conservative American culture is the single most critical reason for the material and military success of the United States. Diamond responded in a *New York Times* article explaining that Romney had misunderstood his argument.[6]

In the academic context, Diamond believes that criticisms of his book are not based on the evidence he assembles but on moral grounds. For example, he thinks the authors of the critical book *Questioning Collapse* "query the interpretation of past societal demises, preferring a positive message about human nature."[7] They "dismiss as an 'accident of geography' those explanations... that rest on environmental factors—such as continental differences in biogeographic endowments,* shapes and locations—but they do not offer a substitute thesis."[8] ("Biogeographic endowments" refers to the distribution of species of plants and animals in a certain area at a specific time.)

While Diamond acknowledges that some societies are resilient enough to survive even extreme crises (an idea strongly advanced in *Questioning Collapse*), he criticizes the authors for illustrating it inappropriately. "For instance, one chapter claims that the Greenland Norse people emigrated rather than dying out, despite no evidence for that claim and despite graphic archaeological evidence of starvation—bones and debris in the topmost archaeological layer from the final winter of the Greenland Western Settlement's existence."[9]

It is rare that any resolution is found in this kind of debate about factual evidence and methodology; the discipline of anthropology has, meanwhile, earned a reputation for uniquely berating Diamond.[10]

1. David Correia, "F**k Jared Diamond," *Capitalism Nature Socialism* 24, no. 4 (2013): 1–6.

2. Penguin Reader's Guide, "A Conversation with Jared Diamond," penguin. com, n.d., accessed September 9, 2015, www.penguin.com/read/book-clubs/collapse/9780143117001.

3. Correia, "F**k Jared Diamond," 4.

4. See, for example: Tony Crook, "Indigenous Human Rights," *Anthropology Today* 14, no. 1 (1998): 18–19.

5. Alex Golub, "Game of Thrones and Anthropology," *Savage Minds*, July 2, 2014, accessed September 10, 2015, http://savageminds. org/2014/07/02/game-of-thrones-and-anthropology/.

6. Jared M. Diamond, "Romney Hasn't Done His Homework," *The New York Times*, August 1, 2012, accessed September 30, 2015, www.nytimes. com/2012/08/02/opinion/mitt-romneys-search-for-simple-answers.html.

7. Jared M. Diamond, "Two Views of Collapse," *Nature* 463, no. 7283 (February 18, 2010): 880.

8. Diamond, "Two Views of Collapse," 880.

9. Diamond, "Two Views of Collapse," 880.

10. Jason Antrosio, "Jared Diamond and Future Public Anthropology," livinganthropologically.com, July 21, 2014, accessed September 10, 2015, www.livinganthropologically.com/2014/07/21/jared-diamond-future-public-anthropology/.

IMPACT AND INFLUENCE TODAY

KEY POINTS

* *Collapse* is an important work for anyone interested in grand narratives of human history. But readers must be aware of the fierce debate that the book has sparked.

* *Collapse* is cited in discussions in many disciplines, including anthropology,* archaeology,* history, and geography. But it has rarely served to clinch any dispute.

* The only point on which all scholars agree is the popularity of *Collapse* among the general public—the result of Diamond's talent for popularizing science. Its influence remains uncontested.

Position

Jared M. Diamond's *Collapse: How Societies Choose to Fail or Survive* may well be a book with wide appeal for anyone interested in great historical sweeps. But readers must be aware of the heated debate that it, and similar works by Diamond, have provoked. Depending on one's take on them, the arguments advanced in *Collapse* can be understood in different ways: from the factually valid to lacking evidence; from the methodologically solid to the theoretically unsustainable; from the politically correct to the morally unacceptable. In particular, the moral and political positions attributed to *Collapse* remain controversial.

One widespread reading of *Collapse* among social scientists is that "Diamond's narrative of disappearance and marginalization is one of conquest's most potent instruments."[1] Also, "*Collapse* focuses on cases of indigenous environmental mismanagement, suggesting that the world's 'have-nots' often wound up that way because they 'chose' to overshoot their environmental limitations and their societies fell apart as a result."[2]

Diamond was explicit in not supporting such a moral or political position. He declared that he wrote *Guns, Germs, and Steel* in order to convince Westerners that European domination is not the result of racial superiority. He wanted to show that Western prosperity depends on factors that have always been at least partly beyond will or merit.

Again, in *Collapse* he maintained this emphasis on environmental factors as a way to demonstrate that any racial explanation is unsubstantial. But he also highlighted the importance of individual action as a way to place more responsibility on actual human beings (as was the case in, for example, the Dominican Republic, where preventative environmental policies were enacted by Rafael Trujillo* and Joaquin Balaguer*).

> *"... a complete roster of potentially relevant variables leads to an unworkably complex model, and Diamond has the virtue of simplicity."*
>
> —— John R. McNeill, "A Usable Past"

Interaction

Collapse, like other works by Diamond, has a bearing on debates concerning a number of disciplines,notably anthropology, archaeology, history, and geography. But these debates do not necessarily end with agreement and eventually run out of energy thanks to the absolute disagreement between Diamond and his critics.

The discussion concerning the factual evidence behind the arguments advanced in *Collapse* has slowly faded, for example, with neither side able to demonstrate that its historical understanding and its use of evidence is superior to the other's. The contributors to the volume *Questioning Collapse* contend that there was never a forest in the Chaco Canyon in New Mexico and that consequently the native Anasazi* could not have deforested what never existed. They further argue that analysis of plant remains in ancient pack-rat middens* (piles of refuse assembled by rodents) there "reveal a climate* and ecology* almost exactly like that which exists today."[3] Diamond, on the other hand, has insisted that "radiocarbon dating of middens revealed a former pinyon-juniper woodland that is now absent from the canyon."[4] Hence, both Diamond and his critics put forward arguments and evidence to support them that remain incompatible. Given this, the debate, confronted by these irreconcilable positions, has tended to stagnate.

The argument concerning environmental determinism* has also come to a halt for precisely the lack of any common ground. For example, historians blame Diamond for not giving enough weight to the role of contingency based on individual decisions and chance. Contrarily, he blames them for denying the role of environmental causes in cultural traits.[5]

While these debates are mostly relevant for an arena of specialists, *Collapse* has also had an undeniable influence on public discussions. Unconcerned by specialist debates, readers have become increasingly interested in such themes as climate change,* environmental damage, cultural relativism (the belief that it is vital to take an individual's culture into account when interpreting his or her actions), and the possibility of learning from the different fates of human societies.[6]

Although these are merits, it can also be argued that Diamond has invited much skepticism from specialists precisely because he insisted on writing for a non-specialist audience.

The Continuing Debate

The debate about *Collapse* and other works by Diamond is ongoing, even if the focus changes constantly. Some critics hone in more on the material in support of Diamond's theory, some on the moral and political implications of the book, some on its theoretical value. But most of these debates tend to stall in the absence of any lack of conclusive evidence to support either side, arguably because the substantial basis of the debate is flawed. While Diamond is caricatured by his critics, it has been argued that his critics, too, "get caricatured by being slotted into one of many already-rehearsed 'you're just' tropes:

- You're just angry because Diamond isn't an anthropologist.
- You're just jealous because Diamond is popular.
- You're just a nitpicking specialist—Diamond is a big-ideas man.
- You're just playing by academic rules—Diamond is an intellectual.
- You're just calling Diamond a determinist, and he isn't a determinist."[7]

Whether as a result of professional envy, charges of oversimplification, lack of further factual evidence, intellectual preferences, or disputed theoretical positions, the debates remain unresolved.

Nevertheless: scholars agree that *Collapse*, as much as other works by Diamond, has had a strong impact on society. This depends primarily on Diamond's writing style, which, as even his critics recognize, engages readers who are otherwise distant from scientific issues. Prompted by Diamond's readability and accessibility, some anthropologists have also made "an effort to shorten that distance,"[8] presumably by making their writing more accessible.

---

1. Michael Wilcox, "Marketing Conquest and the Vanishing Indian: An Indigenous Response to Jared Diamond's Archaeology of the American Southwest," in *Questioning Collapse: Human Resilience, Ecological Vulnerability, and the Aftermath of Empire*, ed. Patricia A. McAnany and Norman Yoffee (New York, NY: Cambridge University Press, 2010), 138.

2. James L. Flexner, "Questioning Collapse: Human Resilience, Ecological Vulnerability, and the Aftermath of Empire," *Pacific Affairs* 84, no. 4 (2011), 741.

3. Jared M. Diamond, "Two Views of Collapse," *Nature* 463, no. 7283 (2010): 880–1.

4. Diamond, "Two Views of Collapse," 881.

5. Jared M. Diamond, "Geographic Determinism: What Does 'Geographic Determinism' Really Mean?," jareddiamond.org, n.d., accessed September 30, 2015, www.jareddiamond.org/Jared_Diamond/Geographic_determinism.html.

6. Mark Lynas, "The Myths of Easter Island—Jared Diamond Responds," marklynas.org, September 22, 2011, accessed September 10, 2015, www.marklynas.org/2011/09/the-myths-of-easter-island-jared-diamond-responds/.

7. Jason Antrosio, "Jared Diamond Won't Beat Mitt Romney—Anthropolitics 2012," livinganthropologically.com, August 4, 2012, accessed September 10, 2015, www.livinganthropologically.com/2012/08/04/diamond-romney/.

8. McAnany and Yoffee, *Questioning Collapse*. See also: Jeremy MacClancy and Chris McDonaugh, eds., *Popularizing Anthropology* (London: Routledge, 2002).

MODULE 12
WHERE NEXT?

KEY POINTS

* Jared Diamond's *Collapse*, a book about societies in many different parts of the world in many different periods, was successful across the globe. Anthropologists* are increasingly anxious to have such an impact themselves. They can no longer ignore or dismiss the fact that such complex questions have been successfully popularized.

* It is unlikely that other scholars will imitate Diamond's intellectual style; most academics still value complexity above accessibility (which might explain why they seldom reach wider audiences).

* *Collapse* advances an argument that concerns humanity as a whole. Grand theories of this kind appeal on a popular level but encounter the skepticism of specialists.

Potential

Collapse: How Societies Choose to Fail or Survive by Jared M. Diamond is a global best seller written by a Pulitzer Prize-winning author, translated into dozens of languages. It has even been turned into a documentary produced in the United States by the National Geographic Society.* A revised edition with an additional chapter on the Cambodian region of Angkor was published in 2011.

It has undeniably left a mark on both the study of societal collapse and on the public debate about climate change* and environmental damage. It is likely to maintain its position and, potentially, influence future scholarship and public discussion, especially because it makes plain the reach of Diamond's approach to big questions for humanity.

What *Collapse* presents, however, is not necessarily new data or methodology. Rather, *Collapse* expands the synthesis of preexisting case studies to the point of offering an unparalleled span of human history, and advances a theoretical argument about the entirety of humankind. It is an example of its author's successful formula: a clear question relevant for humanity as a whole, the comparative method,* and the offer of a succinct answer. Ultimately, it is the popularity of this formula that will grant the text continuing relevance, even though it will also be associated with the many controversies it spurred.

As Diamond's formula has ensured widespread and long-standing success for his books, we might predict that the formula will be applied to future works in pursuit of similar outcomes. In the context of anthropology, to take the example of one discipline among many, scholars have already started to reflect on what they can learn from Diamond to make their own books more widely read and relevant in the public spheres.

For example, in a panel organized at the 2013 meetings of the American Anthropological Association, anthropologists discussed the accessibility of Diamond's work to laypersons, and its resulting relevance for the public debate. This fact suggests that something is changing. Anthropologists increasingly recognize that, although they "shudder at Jared-Diamond-as-Anthropology, it is pretty much standard for how the undergraduate-level audience gets their anthropology and world history."[1] It is undeniable that Diamond's work is now "a primary conduit for how people think they know what they know about culture and cultural relativism"[2] (the belief that, when interpreting an individual's actions and belief, we must take the context of his or her culture into account). For this reason, they think that the "tactic of ignoring Diamond—or... the structures that make a Jared Diamond possible—cannot be sustained."[3]

> "Yes, there is something next, another big book about another big question of human history and human societies. I hope to complete that new book in about another five years. But, as Conan Doyle let Sherlock Holmes explain to Dr. Watson in alluding to the mystery of the giant rat of Sumatra, 'The world is not yet ready for this story.'"
>
> —— Penguin Reader's Guide, "A Conversation with Jared Diamond"

Future Directions

Collapse is an example of Diamond's formula for making academic subjects more accessible to a wider public. Scholars of the humanities and social sciences interested in having an impact on society might want to look at it as a model. Social scientists are increasingly aware of the relevance of this approach, with the Research Excellence Framework, a body that assesses the quality of research in the United Kingdom, considering the impact on "economy, society, public policy, culture and the quality of life" as the main criteria of evaluation.

Even though *Collapse* illustrates one way in which social

sciences can be made more relevant in the public debate, however, it is unlikely that other scholars will imitate Diamond's intellectual style. Social scientists tend to oppose authors who draw conclusions on the basis of broad comparisons. That is particularly true of anthropologists, who reject the possibility of simple answers and emphasize the complexity of sociocultural realities.[4]

Nevertheless, "In contemporary anthropology, pleas for narrative have almost become a cliché... but we rarely get on with actually telling stories. Maybe this is general professional affliction,"[5] wrote the anthropologist Thomas Hylland Eriksen.* In contrast, "Diamond has a gift for storytelling."[6] Anthropologists recognize that it is an ancient and distinctly human desire to tell a story and to tell it well.[7] But notwithstanding these authors' efforts at solving the apparent incompatibility between complexity and narrative, no anthropologist has yet achieved the widespread popularity of Diamond.

Summary

A best seller within days of its publication, *Collapse* was subsequently made into a documentary and provoked debate inside and outside of academia; while its argument, methodology, and theoretical reach—not to mention its political and moral stand— have been questioned, its popular success remains unchallenged.

Indeed, it is precisely its popularity beyond the academic world that has generated so much criticism among specialists. *Collapse* advances an argument about the fate of human societies that concerns humanity in its totality. Grand theories of this kind appeal to the public but rarely win over skeptical specialists.

Another explanation for its popularity outside of academia is Diamond's use of the comparative method. Whatever its appeal to non-specialists, many contemporary scholars see such a method as inappropriate because it overestimates similarities and underestimates differences.

Finally, however, whether you agree with Diamond or not, the impact of his books remains beyond dispute.

---

1. Jason Antrosio, "Jared Diamond and Future Public Anthropology," livinganthropologically.com, July 21, 2014, accessed September 10, 2015, www.livinganthropologically.com/2014/07/21/jared-diamond-future-public-anthropology/.

2. Antrosio, "Jared Diamond."

3. Antrosio, "Jared Diamond."

4. Antrosio, "Jared Diamond."

5. Thomas H. Eriksen, *Engaging Anthropology: The Case for a Public Presence* (Oxford, UK; New York, NY: Berg, 2006).

6. Bryn Williams, "Can You Trust Jared Diamond?" *Slate*, February 18, 2013, accessed September 30, 2015, www.slate.com/articles/health_and_ science/books/2013/02/jared_diamond_the_world_until_yesterday_ anthropologists_are_wary_of_lack.html.

7. Patricia A. McAnany and Norman Yoffee, eds., *Questioning Collapse: Human Resilience, Ecological Vulnerability, and the Aftermath of Empire* (New York, NY: Cambridge University Press, 2010), 1.

 **GLOSSARY OF TERMS**

1. **Anasazi:** a term originating in the Navajo language, indicating the ancient inhabitants of the territory comprising contemporary southern Utah, northern Arizona, northwestern New Mexico, and southwestern Colorado. Current consensus dates their origin to around the twelfth century B.C.E. In *Collapse*, Diamond deals with different Anasazi groups and cultures that collapsed between the twelfth and fifteenth centuries B.C.E.

2. **Anthropology:** the study of humankind. It breaks down into multiple subfields, each focusing on one specific aspect, such as culture, social institutions, language, biology, and economy, among others.

3. **Archaeology:** the scientific study of past human activity by means of the examination of ancient bones, artifacts, and environmental modifications.

4. **Axiology:** a theory of value—that is, of all things that a particular group of people considers valuable. In the context of the societies studied by Diamond, the values of a society determined a people's ability to overcome societal collapse.

5. **Biodiversity:** the measure indicating the number and variety of organisms (both animal and vegetal) in a given ecosystem. It varies across the globe and determines a variety of advantages for local inhabitants. For example, greater biodiversity increases fodder yield, crop yield, and wood production.

6. **Biogeographic endowment:** the distribution of species of plants and animals in a geographic space at a particular time.

7. **Biophysics:** a discipline that studies biological systems, such as the human body, with methods borrowed from physics.

8. **Botany:** the scientific study of plants.

9. **Chiefdoms:** an independent political organization in which status is granted as a consequence of belonging to a descent group. Individuals are ranked on the basis of their kinship proximity to a paramount chief.

10. **Climate:** the long-term, large-scale pattern of variation in meteorological variables such as temperature, precipitation, wind, and humidity. It differs from weather, which indicates the short-term pattern of variation in meteorological variables in a relatively smaller location.

11. **Climate change:** the long-term, large-scale fluctuation in climate: decades of drought, a century of wet weather, or the Little Ice Age of the seventeenth to the nineteenth centuries. Today this term, which Diamond uses consistently throughout *Collapse*, is often taken to mean "catastrophic anthropogenic (human-activated) global warming." Climate change is not exclusively caused by human beings, however, and also occurs thanks to natural causes; moreover, it does not necessarily result in a warmer climate, but one that can be colder, wetter, drier, and more or less variable.

12. **Comparative environmental history:** an expression used by Diamond to indicate a method for studying human societies, which consists of comparing in-depth case studies of different societies in order to isolate key variables that provide general explanations.

13. **Comparative method:** a method of research and analysis that consists of the examination of two or more cases and identifying similarities and differences that might explain their respective outcomes.

14. **Continental axis:** an imaginary line traced horizontally on a continent whose territory extends for longer from east to west than from north to south. Vice versa, the line is traced vertically if the territory of a continent extends for longer from north to south than from east to west.

15. **Cultural imperialism:** the imposition by a dominant group of a particular culture upon a dominated group. It can take various forms, ranging from military control to indoctrination.

16. **Cultural possibilism:** a theory in geography that says culture is shaped by social rather than environmental conditions. It follows that its approach is directly opposed to geographical determinism.

17. **Deforestation:** the removal of trees from a given territory. The main cause of deforestation is agriculture, including subsistence farming, commercial agriculture, and logging.

18. **Ecology:** the scientific study of the relations between organisms and their habitat. Ecologists advocate the sustainable management of environmental resources through changes in public policies and individual behavior.

19. **Empiricism:** a theory of knowledge that considers direct observation as the sole method of obtaining reliable knowledge.

20. **Environmental degradation:** the deterioration of an ecosystem due to the progressive exhaustion of its resources. It results in the depletion of air, water, and soil quality and the extinction of wildlife.

21. **Environmental determinism:** a theory suggesting that the environment determines the historical trajectories (paths) of a society associated with a particular territory. Its extreme tenets hold that individual actions cannot substantially alter the influence of environmental factors—such as climate, fauna (animals), flora (plants), and continental axis—on the fate of a society.

22. **Environmental history:** the scientific study of the relationship between human societies and their environment through time.

23. **Erosion:** the movement of soil and rock from one location to another, caused by such factors as rain, wind, agriculture, and deforestation. One major consequence of erosion is land degradation, which in turn decreases soil fertility.

24. **Ethnocentrism:** a tendency to adopt one's own cultural theories and values to examine and evaluate other people's cultures. Generally, ethnocentrism implies that one's own culture is somehow superior to the culture of other people.

25. **Ethnography:** the scientific study of groups of people, along with their customs, habits, and beliefs.

26. **Geographic determinism:** see Environmental determinism.

27. **Globalization:** the process of increasing interconnectedness among the people of the world, characterized by increasingly rapid and frequent travel, communications, and material exchanges.

28. **Hard sciences:** a popular expression that is often used to indicate the natural or physical sciences. Disciplines such as chemistry, biology, and physics are considered "hard sciences" by virtue of their usage of hypotheses and experiments as methodologies to understand the universe.

29. **Hypertrophy:** a term borrowed from medicine to indicate the excessive growth of a system or structure.

30. **Idiographic approach:** the idea that no phenomena can be comparable. It encourages the description of concrete properties, not the abstraction of general ideas or laws.

31. **Immobilism:** the inability or unwillingness to take political action, often a result of conservative values.

32. **Independent variable:** an expression borrowed from mathematics to indicate the external cause of a phenomenon.

33. **Interdisciplinarity:** a combination of different academic disciplines in a single research activity. It differs from multidisciplinarity in that it synthesizes multiple disciplines into a new kind of research activity rather than solving a particular research problem with many separate contributions.

34. **Laboratory conditions:** the absence of external interference in a controlled environment in which a phenomenon is scientifically studied.

35. **Little Ice Age:** a period of the Earth's climatic history that took place from about 1400 c.e. to 1800. During this time, the mean temperature in the Northern Hemisphere decreased considerably.

36. **Malthusian trap:** the theory, proposed by the English economist and demographer Thomas Malthus, that the exponential growth of human populations tends to outrun the arithmetic growth of food production.

37. **Midden:** a concentration of ancient waste products left in a particular location. These heaps of remains, excrement, and all sorts of old material are extremely useful for archaeologists who study past societies.

38. **Multicausative:** a term indicating a fact that results from multiple causes which combine with each other. Diamond's theory, for example, is multicausative because it explains societal collapses as resulting from the combination of five collapse factors.

39. **Multidisciplinarity:** an approach that involves contributions from multiple disciplines for the sake of addressing complex problems that one single discipline can only partially help to solve or describe.

40. ***National Geographic***: the journal of the US National Geographic Society,

published continuously since 1888.

41. **Natural experiment:** the observation of a context (such as a group of people in a given territory) exposed to influences beyond the control of the investigators, who attempt to establish causal connections between the exposure and the changes in the object of study.

42. **Nomothetic approach:** an idea suggesting the possibility of abstracting general ideas or laws from a set of particular facts. The term "nomothetic" is often opposed to "idiographic".

43. **Ornithology:** the systematic, scientific study of birds.

44. **Per capita income:** a measure of the average income earned by a person in a given territory, calculated by dividing the total income in the area by the total population.

45. **Photosynthetic capacity:** the amount of sunlight per acre that the Earth is able to absorb. Regardless of the quantity of light produced by the sun, there is a maximum amount that can be absorbed. That means that, if man-made areas absorb most of the sunlight, there is not much sunlight left for natural ecosystems.

46. **Physiology:** a subdiscipline of biology that studies the normal functioning of living organisms.

47. **Pollen and charcoal analysis:** a method of determining the presence of species of plants in a given territory through the analysis of their remains.

48. **Polymath:** a person with a multiplicity of interests and in-depth knowledge in a diversity of disciplines. Often, polymaths combine theoretical and practical knowledge with the ability to speak multiple languages and play numerous instruments.

49. **Postclassic period:** a period of Mesoamerican history from about 950 to 1539 c.e.

50. **Pre-Columbian Maya:** a Mesoamerican civilization developed before 2000 B.C.E. in the area encompassing southeastern Mexico, Guatemala, Belize, the western part of El Salvador, and Honduras. It collapsed partly because of the drought caused by cutting trees to the point of irreversible deforestation. This

altered the local water cycling and decreased rainfalls, resulting in a protracted drought.

51. **Radiocarbon dating:** a method that determines the age of an object by measuring the quantity of radiocarbon, a radioactive isotope of carbon, it contains. Since the quantity of radiocarbon in an animal or plant decreases constantly after death, it is possible to calculate approximately when the animal or plant died.

52. **Reforestation:** an increase in the number of living trees per acre as a consequence of human intentional plantation or natural growth in a previously deforested area.

53. **Resilience:** the ability of a system, such as a society or living organism, to cope with changes and challenges. For example, climate resilience indicates the capacity of an ecological context or human society to adapt to long-term changes in temperature or humidity.

54. **Rwanda:** an east-central equatorial African nation; from April to July 1994, it saw the massacre of some 500,000–1,000,000 people, the greatest majority of whom were of the Tutsi ethnic group, at the hands of members of the Hutu ethnic group.

55. **Salinization:** an increase in the presence of salt in the soil. The consequences of salinization include reduced plant growth and yield, reduced water quality, and increased soil erosion.

56. **Social Darwinism:** a group of theories that explain human phenomena in terms of evolution, natural selection, and survival of the fittest. The expression derives from Charles Darwin's theory of natural selection, which was not initially meant to be applied to sociocultural issues. Critics of racist and imperialist views that nature makes "winners" and "losers" invented this term.

57 **Sustainability:** the ability to make use of environmental resources without exhausting them or damaging the environment.

58. **Tokugawa Japan:** a period of Japanese history in which Japanese society was ruled by the Tokugawa shogunate, a feudal military government that lasted from 1603 to 1868.

59. **Water management:** the ability to use water resources without exhausting them, reducing their qualities, or damaging the environment.

60. **Western imperialism:** an expression that roughly indicates the ideology justifying the rule of European powers over large territories in Africa, Oceania, and the Americas. Such justification is often given in racial terms, whereby these continents should not be controlled and governed by their inhabitants, but by those who, by virtue of racial superiority, can do so more efficiently.

PEOPLE MENTIONED IN THE TEXT

1. **Aristotle (384–322 B.C.E.)** was a philosopher and scientist at Plato's Academy in ancient Athens, Greece. He explained the cultural differences between Northern Europeans,Asians, and Greeks as caused by different climatic conditions.

2. **Paul Bahn** is a British archaeologist, translator, writer, and broadcaster who has published extensively on a range of archaeological topics, including *The Enigmas of Easter Island* (with John Flenley, 2003).

3. **Joaquin Balaguer (1906–2002)** was the president of the Dominican Republic for three non-consecutive terms between 1960 and 1996.

4. **Franz Boas (1858–1942)** was a Prussian-born anthropologist who has been called the "father of American anthropology." He rejected evolutionary approaches to the study of culture and promoted historical particularism and cultural relativism.

5. **Mark Brenner** is a limnologist and paleolimnologist (scholar of bodies of water such as rivers and lakes), with special interests in tropical and subtropical lakes and watersheds. He reconstructs the history of aquatic ecosystems on the basis of sediment cores from the bottoms of lakes.

6. **David Correia (b. 1968)** is an American scholar and activist, and an associate professor of American studies at the University of New Mexico.

7. **George Cowgill (1929–2018)** was an American anthropologist and archaeologist with fieldwork experience in Teotihuacán, Mexico. He contributed to the comparative study of ancient states and cities with numerous publications.

8. **Jason H. Curtis** works as a senior associate in geochemistry at the University of Florida and is an expert in climatic variation in ancient societies.

9. **Thomas Hylland Eriksen (b. 1962)** is a Norwegian professor of social anthropology at the University of Oslo and currently president of the European Association of Social Anthropologists. One of his research interests focuses on the popularization of social anthropology.

10. **Frederick K. Errington** is emeritus professor of anthropology at Trinity College, with research experience in Papua New Guinea, Sumatra, and Montana. Much of his work is done in collaboration with his wife Deborah Gewertz.

11. **Brian Fagan (b. 1936)** is an archaeologist and anthropologist with fieldwork experience in Africa.

12. **John Flenley** is emeritus professor in biogeography at Massey University, New Zealand and a palynologist (a specialist in "dust"—pollen and spores). He has published prolifically in the field of paleopalynology.

13. **Alex Golub** is an anthropologist with fieldwork experience in Papua New Guinea. He is the founder of the popular cultural anthropology website savageminds.org, which has long engaged with the work of Jared Diamond.

14. **Hippocrates (460–370 B.C.E.)** is referred to as the "father of Western medicine." He believed the environment was responsible for major features of human character, body, and culture.

15. **David A. Hodell (b. 1958)** is a geologist and paleoclimatologist working as professor of geology at the University of Cambridge. His research with Brenner, Curtis, and Guilderson focused on the collapse of the Maya Empire.

16. **Terry Hunt** is an archaeologist and a professor of anthropology at the University of Oregon. His research focuses on environmental change and life on the islands of the Pacific Ocean. He has published extensively in the fields of Pacific archaeology, prehistory, and linguistics.

17. **Carl Lipo** is an archaeologist who has done research on prehistoric potters of the Mississippi Valley and the construction of the famous Easter Island's moai.

18. **Marcel Mauss (1872–1950)** was a French sociologist, although he is best known for his anthropological book *The Gift* (1925), which compares the circulation of objects in different past and present societies.

19. **Patricia A. McAnany (b.1953)** is a Kenan eminent professor of anthropology, University of North Carolina, who conducted archaeological research in the Maya region and currently runs heritage programs with contemporary Maya communities.

20. **Bonnie J. McCay** is professor emerita of anthropology at Rutgers University.

21. **Thomas McGovern** is a professor with specialization in the fields of environmental and island archaeology and climate change.

22. **John Robert McNeill (b. 1954)** is professor of environmental history at Georgetown University. His most famous book is *Something New Under the Sun:An Environmental History of the Twentieth-Century World* (2000).

23. **Montesquieu, Charles-Louis de Secondat, Baron de La Brède et de Montesquieu (1689–1755)** was a French lawyer and political philosopher. In *The Spirit of the Laws* he argued that climate might substantially influence the features of man and society.

24. **Dick Peet (b. 1940)** is a professor of human geography at Clark University and founder of the journal *Antipode*. He works in politics and ecology.

25. **Benny Peiser (b. 1957)** is a social anthropologist at Liverpool John Moores University. He is the director of the Global Warming Policy Foundation.

26. **Plato (c. 424–c.348 B.C.E.)** was a philosopher and mathematician, a student of Socrates, and regarded by some as the "father of philosophy."

27. **William Rees (b. 1943)** is a professor at the University of British Columbia with research interests in global environmental trends, climate change, and sustainable socioeconomic development.

28. **James Robinson (b. 1960)** is an economist and political scientist currently holding a position of professor at the University of Chicago. With Daron Acemoğlu, he wrote *Why Nations Fail:The Origins of Power, Prosperity and Poverty* (2012). With Jared Diamond, he wrote *Natural Experiments of History* (2010).

29. **Mitt Romney (b. 1947)** is an American businessman and Republican politician. He was defeated in the November 2012 presidential election by Democratic President Barack Obama.

30. **Claire Russell (1919–99)** was a psychotherapist, poet, and wife of William M. S. Russell, with whom she worked and published on subjects as diverse as psychoanalysis, animal behavior, and the collapse of ancient civilizations.

31. **William M. S. Russell (1925–2006)** was an emeritus professor at Reading University, and the author, with his wife Claire, of *The Myths of Greece and Rome* (2000) and *Population Crisis and Population Cycles* (1999).

32. **Carl Ortwin Sauer (1889–1975)** was an American emeritus professor of geography at the University of California at Berkeley. One of his most important contributions to the discipline was his firm criticism of environmental determinism.

33. **Joseph Tainter (b. 1949)** is an American anthropologist and historian. He is known for his book *The Collapse of Complex Societies* (1988), which compares the collapse of the Maya, the Chaco, and the Roman Empire.

34. **Rafael Trujillo (1891–1961)** was the ruler of the Dominican Republic from 1930 to 1961. His time in power was characterized by top-down violence and repression. However, it brought an era of general stability and economic prosperity.

35. **Andrew P. Vayda (b. 1931)** is professor emeritus of anthropology and ecology at Rutgers University and founder of the academic journal *Human Ecology*.

36. **Mike V. Wilcox** is associate professor of anthropology at Stanford University. His field of expertise includes the culture and archaeology of the American Southwest. His publications are critical of Diamond's work.

37. **Norman Yoffee (b.1944)** is an Assyriologist (a scholar of the ancient Near Eastern empire of Assyria) and anthropologist who conducted research and published on the Old Babylonian period and the rise and fall of ancient states in comparative perspective.

 **WORKS CITED**

1. Antrosio, Jason. "Jared Diamond and Future Public Anthropology." livinganthropologically.com, July 21, 2014. Accessed September 10, 2015. www.livinganthropologically.com/2014/07/21/jared-diamond-future-public-anthropology/.

2. "Jared Diamond Won't Beat Mitt Romney—Anthropolitics 2012." livinganthropologically.com, August 4, 2012. Accessed September 10, 2015. www.livinganthropologically.com/2012/08/04/diamond-romney/.

3. Blaut, James M. "Environmentalism and Eurocentrism." *Geographical Review* 89, no. 3 (1999): 391–408.

4. Butzer, Karl W. "Cultural Ecology." In *Geography in America*, edited by Gary L. Gaile and Cort J. Willmott, 192–208. Columbus: Merrill, 1989.

5. Correia, David. "F**k Jared Diamond." *Capitalism Nature Socialism* 24, no. 4 (2013): 1–6.

6. Crook, Tony. "Indigenous Human Rights." *Anthropology Today* 14, no. 1 (1998): 18–19.

7. Diamond, Jared M. "About Me." jareddiamond.org, n.d. Accessed September 30, 2015. www.jareddiamond.org/Jared_Diamond/About_Me.html.

8. *Collapse: How Societies Choose to Fail or Survive*. London: Penguin, 2011.

9. "Concentrating Activity of the Gall-bladder." PhD diss. University of Cambridge, 1961.

10. "Easter's End." *Discover Magazine*, August 1995.

11. "Geographic Determinism: What Does 'Geographic Determinism' Really Mean?." jareddiamond.org, n.d. Accessed September 30, 2015. www.jareddiamond.org/Jared_Diamond/Geographic_determinism.html.

12. *Guns, Germs, and Steel*. London: Random House, 2013.

13. "The Last Americans: Environmental Collapse and the End of Civilization." *Harper's Magazine*, June 2003.

14. "Romney Hasn't Done His Homework." *The New York Times*, August 1, 2012. Accessed September 30, 2015. www.nytimes.com/2012/08/02/opinion/mitt-

romneys-search-for-simple-answers.html.

15. "Paradise Lost." *Discover Magazine*, November 1997.

16. *The Third Chimpanzee: The Evolution and Future of the Human Animal.* London: HarperCollins, 2006.

17. "Two Views of Collapse." *Nature* 463, no. 7283 (February 18, 2010): 880–1.

18. *Why Is Sex Fun?: The Evolution Of Human Sexuality*. London: Hachette, 2014.

19. *The World Until Yesterday: What Can We Learn from Traditional Societies?* New York: Viking, 2013.

20. Diamond, Jared M., K. David Bishop, and James D. Gilardi. "Geophagy in New Guinea Birds." *Ibis* 141, no. 2 (1999): 181–93.

21. Diamond, Jared M., and James A. Robinson, eds. *Natural Experiments of History*. Cambridge, MA: Harvard University Press, 2010.

22. Eriksen, Thomas H. *Engaging Anthropology: The Case for a Public Presence.* Oxford, UK; New York, NY: Berg, 2006.

23. Esty, Amos. "An Interview with Jared Diamond." *American Scientist Online*, n.d. Accessed September 30, 2015. www.americanscientist.org/bookshelf/pub/jared-diamond.

24. Fagan, Brian. *Floods, Famines, and Emperors: El Niño and the Fate of Civilizations*. New York: Basic Books, 1999.

25. Flexner, James L. "Questioning Collapse: Human Resilience, Ecological Vulnerability, and the Aftermath of Empire." *Pacific Affairs* 84, no. 4 (2011): 740–2.

26. Friedman, Kerim. "From the Archives: Savage Minds vs. Jared Diamond." *Savage Minds*, January 22, 2012. Accessed September 30, 2015. http://savageminds.org/2012/01/22/from-the-archives-savage-minds-vs-jared-diamond/.

27. Golub, Alex. "Game of Thrones and Anthropology." *Savage Minds*, July 2, 2014. Accessed September 10, 2015. http://savageminds.org/2014/07/02/game-of-thrones-and-anthropology/.

28. Harris, Marvin. *Cultural Materialism: The Struggle for a Science of Culture.* New York: Random House, 1979.

29. Hodell, David A., Jason H. Curtis, and Mark Brenner. "Possible Role of Climate in the Collapse of Classic Maya Civilization." *Nature* 375, no. 6530 (1995): 391–4.

30. Hunt, Terry, and Carl Lipo. "Ecological Catastrophe, Collapse, and the Myth of 'Ecocide' on Rapa Nui (Easter Island)." In *Questioning Collapse: Human Resilience, Ecological Vulnerability, and the Aftermath of Empire,* edited by Patricia A. McAnany and Norman Yoffee, 223–46. New York, NY: Cambridge University Press, 2010.

31. Ingold, Tim. "Introduction to Culture." In *Companion Encyclopedia of Anthropology*, edited by Tim Ingold, 329–49. London and New York: Routledge, 1994.

32. Johnson, George. "A Question of Blame When Societies Fall." *The New York Times*, December 25, 2007. Accessed September 30, 2015. www.nytimes.com/2007/12/25/science/25diam.html.

33. Judkins, Gabriel, Marissa Smith, and Eric Keys. "Determinism within Human—Environment Research and the Rediscovery of Environmental Causation." *The Geographical Journal* 174, no. 1 (2008): 17–29.

34. Kennedy, Donald. "The Choice: Finding Hope in the History of Environmental Ruin." *Foreign Affairs* 84, no. 2 (2005): 134–8.

35. Lynas, Mark. "The Myths of Easter Island—Jared Diamond Responds." marklynas.org, September 22, 2011. Accessed September 10, 2015. www.marklynas.org/2011/09/the-myths-of-easter-island-jared-diamond-responds/.

36. McAnany, Patricia A., and Norman Yoffee, eds. *Questioning Collapse: Human Resilience, Ecological Vulnerability, and the Aftermath of Empire.* New York, NY: Cambridge University Press, 2010.

37. MacClancy, Jeremy, and Chris McDonaugh, eds. *Popularizing Anthropology.* London: Routledge, 2002.

38. McGovern, Thomas, Gerald Bigelow, Thomas Amorosi, and Daniel Russell.

"Northern Islands, Human Error, and Environmental Degradation: A View of Social and Ecological Change in the Medieval North Atlantic." *Human Ecology* 16, no. 3 (1988): 225–70.

39. McMichael, Anthony J. "Collapse. How Societies Choose to Fail or Succeed. Jared Diamond." *International Journal of Epidemiology* 35, no. 2 (2006): 499–500.

40. McMillan, Stephanie. "The Buying and Selling of Jared Diamond." counterpunch.org, December 12, 2009. Accessed September 9, 2015. www.counterpunch.org/2009/12/08/the-buying-and-selling-of-jared-diamond/.

41. McNeill, John R. "A Usable Past." *American Scientist* 93, no. 2 (2005): 172–5.

42. Peiser, Benny. "From Genocide to Ecocide: The Rape of Rapa Nui." *Energy & Environment* 16, no. 3 (2005): 513–40.

43. Penguin Reader's Guide, "A Conversation with Jared Diamond." penguin.com, n.d. Accessed September 9, 2015. www.penguin.com/read/book-clubs/collapse/9780143117001.

44. Rappaport, Roy A. *Pigs for the Ancestors: Ritual in the Ecology of a New Guinea People.* New Haven: Yale University Press, 1968.

45. Rees, William. "Contemplating the Abyss." Nature 433, no. 7021 (2005): 15–16.

46. Russell, Claire, and William M. S. Russell. "Population Crises and Population Cycles." *Medicine, Conflict and Survival* 16, no. 4 (2000): 383–410.

47. Tainter, Joseph. *The Collapse of Complex Societies.* Cambridge: Cambridge University Press, 1988.

48. Tett, Gillian. "The Science Interview: Jared Diamond." *Financial Times*, October 11, 2013. Accessed September 30, 2015. www.ft.com/intl/cms/s/2/1f786618-307a-11e3-80a4-00144feab7de.html#axzz3jQUrhdub.

49. Vayda, Andrew P., and Bonnie J. McCay. "New Directions in Ecology and Ecological Anthropology." *Annual Review of Anthropology* 4 (1975): 293–306.

50. Wilcox, Michael. "Marketing Conquest and the Vanishing Indian: An Indigenous Response to Jared Diamond's Archaeology of the American Southwest." In

Questioning Collapse: Human Resilience, Ecological Vulnerability, and the Aftermath of Empire, edited by Patricia A. McAnany and Norman Yoffee, 113–41. New York, NY: Cambridge University Press, 2010.

51. Williams, Bryn. "Can You Trust Jared Diamond?" *Slate*, February 18, 2013. Accessed September 30, 2015. www.slate.com/articles/health_and_science/ books/2013/02/jared_diamond_the_world_until_yesterday_anthropologists_are_ wary_of_lack.html.

52. Yoffee, Norman and George Cowgill, eds. *The Collapse of Ancient States and Civilizations.* Tucson: University of Arizona Press, 1988.

原书作者简介

贾雷德·M.戴蒙德1937年生于美国波士顿。他运用生物学、人类学、生态学、地理学等多种学科方法研究人类历史。戴蒙德早年在哈佛大学学习生物化学，之后在剑桥大学学习生理学，却在1964年前往新几内亚后对生态学产生了兴趣。之后，他又对环境史产生兴趣，而现在他是加利福尼亚大学洛杉矶分校的地理学教授，也是环境活动家和畅销书作家。凭借《枪炮、病菌与钢铁》（1997）这本颇具争议的著作，他获得了著名的普利策奖。

本书作者简介

鲁道夫·马乔博士获伦敦政治经济学院人类学硕士学位和曼彻斯特大学社会人类学博士学位，现任牛津大学精神病学院博士后研究员。

世界名著中的批判性思维

《世界思想宝库钥匙丛书》致力于深入浅出地阐释全世界著名思想家的观点，不论是谁、在何处都能了解到，从而推进批判性思维发展。

《世界思想宝库钥匙丛书》与世界顶尖大学的一流学者合作，为一系列学科中最有影响的著作推出新的分析文本，介绍其观点和影响。在这一不断扩展的系列中，每种选入的著作都代表了历经时间考验的思想典范。通过为这些著作提供必要背景、揭示原作者的学术渊源以及说明这些著作所产生的影响，本系列图书希望让读者以新视角看待这些划时代的经典之作。读者应学会思考、运用并挑战这些著作中的观点，而不是简单接受它们。

ABOUT THE AUTHOR OF THE ORIGINAL WORK

Born in Boston in the United States in 1937, **Jared M. Diamond** studies human history using a wide-ranging multidisciplinary approach that draws on biology, anthropology, ecology, and geography. Diamond first trained as a biochemist at Harvard University and as a physiologist at Cambridge, but became interested in ecology when he visited New Guinea in 1964. He then developed an interest in environmental history, and is now professor of geography at the University of California, Los Angeles, as well as an environmental activist and popular writer. He won the prestigious Pulitzer Prize for his controversial 1997 work *Guns, Germs, and Steel.*

ABOUT THE AUTHOR OF THE ANALYSIS

Dr Rodolfo Maggio holds a masters degree in anthropology from the London School of Economics and a PhD in social anthropology from the University of Manchester. He is currently a postdoctoral researcher in the Department of Psychiatry at the University of Oxford.

ABOUT MACAT
GREAT WORKS FOR CRITICAL THINKING

Macat is focused on making the ideas of the world's great thinkers accessible and comprehensible to everybody, everywhere, in ways that promote the development of enhanced critical thinking skills.

It works with leading academics from the world's top universities to produce new analyses that focus on the ideas and the impact of the most influential works ever written across a wide variety of academic disciplines. Each of the works that sit at the heart of its growing library is an enduring example of great thinking. But by setting them in context — and looking at the influences that shaped their authors, as well as the responses they provoked — Macat encourages readers to look at these classics and game-changers with fresh eyes. Readers learn to think, engage and challenge their ideas, rather than simply accepting them.

批判性思维与《大崩溃：社会如何选择兴亡》

首要批判性思维技巧：阐释

次要批判性思维技巧：理性化思维

美国学者贾雷德·M.戴蒙德在《大崩溃：社会如何选择兴亡》一书中有效运用了他的阐释能力。该书旨在探索存活社会和衰亡社会表征背后的意义。

例如，为何10世纪初殖民格陵兰岛的斯堪的纳维亚的诺尔斯人没能存活，而新几内亚高地人却得以存活？戴蒙德通过分析手头的证据发现，社会崩溃的前兆往往是人口急剧减少，以及政治、经济和社会复杂程度显著下降。戴蒙德继续深入挖掘，提炼出决定各历史时期人类社会兴亡的五个主要因素：环境退化（生态系统因资源枯竭而退化）、气候变化（自然或人为）、强邻在侧、贸易伙伴弱化以及社会能否获得应对挑战所需的资源。

戴蒙德研究的广度提供了认识这些概念的基础，但也难免带来了复杂的疑问：如此多不同学科的专家提出的证据如何能加以对比？戴蒙德对于手头证据意义的理解能力——以及必要时探究并澄清意义的意识——是其成就的基石，并示范了阐释技巧如何构建坚实的批判性思维框架。

CRITICAL THINKING AND *COLLAPSE*

- Primary critical thinking skill: INTERPRETATION
- Secondary critical thinking skill: REASONING

American scholar Jared M. Diamond deploys his powers of interpretation to great effect in *Collapse: How Societies Choose to Fail or Survive* which seeks to understand the meaning behind the available evidence describing societies that have survived and those that have withered and died.

Why, for example, did the Norsemen of Scandinavia who colonized Greenland in the early tenth century not survive, while the inhabitants of Highland New Guinea did? With the evidence to hand, Diamond notes that a society's collapse tends to be preceded by a severe reduction in population and considerable decreases in political, economic and social complexity. Delving even deeper, Diamond isolates five major factors determine the success or failure of human societies in all periods of history: environmental degradation, which occurs when an ecosystem deteriorates as its resources are exhausted; climate change (natural or man-made); hostile neighbors; weakened trading partners; and access or otherwise to the resources that enable the society to adapt its challenges.

The breadth of Diamond's research provides the springboard from which to reach these definitions, but it inevitably also introduces complications; how can evidence produced by specialists in so many different disciplines be compared? Diamond's ability to understand the meaning of the evidence at hand—and his readiness to seek and supply clarifications of meaning where necessary—underpin his achievement, and comprise a textbook example of how interpretative skills can provide a framework for strong critical thinking.

《世界思想宝库钥匙丛书》简介

　　《世界思想宝库钥匙丛书》致力于为一系列在各领域产生重大影响的人文社科类经典著作提供独特的学术探讨。每一本读物都不仅仅是原经典著作的内容摘要，而是介绍并深入研究原经典著作的学术渊源、主要观点和历史影响。这一丛书的目的是提供一套学习资料，以促进读者掌握批判性思维，从而更全面、深刻地去理解重要思想。

　　每一本读物分为 3 个部分：学术渊源、学术思想和学术影响，每个部分下有 4 个小节。这些章节旨在从各个方面研究原经典著作及其反响。

　　由于独特的体例，每一本读物不但易于阅读，而且另有一项优点：所有读物的编排体例相同，读者在进行某个知识层面的调查或研究时可交叉参阅多本该丛书中的相关读物，从而开启跨领域研究的路径。

　　为了方便阅读，每本读物最后还列出了术语表和人名表（在书中则以星号 * 标记），此外还有参考文献。

　　《世界思想宝库钥匙丛书》与剑桥大学合作，理清了批判性思维的要点，即如何通过 6 种技能来进行有效思考。其中 3 种技能让我们能够理解问题，另 3 种技能让我们有能力解决问题。这 6 种技能合称为"批判性思维 PACIER 模式"，它们是：

分析：了解如何建立一个观点；
评估：研究一个观点的优点和缺点；
阐释：对意义所产生的问题加以理解；
创造性思维：提出新的见解，发现新的联系；
解决问题：提出切实有效的解决办法；
理性化思维：创建有说服力的观点。

THE MACAT LIBRARY

The Macat Library is a series of unique academic explorations of seminal works in the humanities and social sciences — books and papers that have had a significant and widely recognised impact on their disciplines. It has been created to serve as much more than just a summary of what lies between the covers of a great book. It illuminates and explores the influences on, ideas of, and impact of that book. Our goal is to offer a learning resource that encourages critical thinking and fosters a better, deeper understanding of important ideas.

Each publication is divided into three Sections: Influences, Ideas, and Impact. Each Section has four Modules. These explore every important facet of the work, and the responses to it.

This Section-Module structure makes a Macat Library book easy to use, but it has another important feature. Because each Macat book is written to the same format, it is possible (and encouraged!) to cross-reference multiple Macat books along the same lines of inquiry or research. This allows the reader to open up interesting interdisciplinary pathways.

To further aid your reading, lists of glossary terms and people mentioned are included at the end of this book (these are indicated by an asterisk [*] throughout) — as well as a list of works cited.

Macat has worked with the University of Cambridge to identify the elements of critical thinking and understand the ways in which six different skills combine to enable effective thinking.

Three allow us to fully understand a problem; three more give us the tools to solve it. Together, these six skills make up the PACIER model of critical thinking. They are:

ANALYSIS — understanding how an argument is built
EVALUATION — exploring the strengths and weaknesses of an argument
INTERPRETATION — understanding issues of meaning
CREATIVE THINKING — coming up with new ideas and fresh connections
PROBLEM-SOLVING — producing strong solutions
REASONING — creating strong arguments

"《世界思想宝库钥匙丛书》提供了独一无二的跨学科学习和研究工具。它介绍那些革新了各自学科研究的经典著作,还邀请全世界一流专家和教育机构进行严谨的分析,为每位读者打开世界顶级教育的大门。"

—— 安德烈亚斯·施莱歇尔,
经济合作与发展组织教育与技能司司长

"《世界思想宝库钥匙丛书》直面大学教育的巨大挑战……他们组建了一支精干而活跃的学者队伍,来推出在研究广度上颇具新意的教学材料。"

—— 布罗尔斯教授、勋爵,剑桥大学前校长

"《世界思想宝库钥匙丛书》的愿景令人赞叹。它通过分析和阐释那些曾深刻影响人类思想以及社会、经济发展的经典文本,提供了新的学习方法。它推动批判性思维,这对于任何社会和经济体来说都是至关重要的。这就是未来的学习方法。"

—— 查尔斯·克拉克阁下,英国前教育大臣

"对于那些影响了各自领域的著作,《世界思想宝库钥匙丛书》能让人们立即了解到围绕那些著作展开的评论性言论,这让该系列图书成为在这些领域从事研究的师生们不可或缺的资源。"

—— 威廉·特朗佐教授,加利福尼亚大学圣地亚哥分校

"Macat offers an amazing first-of-its-kind tool for interdisciplinary learning and research. Its focus on works that transformed their disciplines and its rigorous approach, drawing on the world's leading experts and educational institutions, opens up a world-class education to anyone."

—— Andreas Schleicher, Director for Education and Skills, Organisation for Economic Co-operation and Development

"Macat is taking on some of the major challenges in university education... They have drawn together a strong team of active academics who are producing teaching materials that are novel in the breadth of their approach."

—— Prof Lord Broers, former Vice-Chancellor of the University of Cambridge

"The Macat vision is exceptionally exciting. It focuses upon new modes of learning which analyse and explain seminal texts which have profoundly influenced world thinking and so social and economic development. It promotes the kind of critical thinking which is essential for any society and economy. This is the learning of the future."

—— Rt Hon Charles Clarke, former UK Secretary of State for Education

"The Macat analyses provide immediate access to the critical conversation surrounding the books that have shaped their respective discipline, which will make them an invaluable resource to all of those, students and teachers, working in the field."

—— Prof William Tronzo, University of California at San Diego

♚ The Macat Library
世界思想宝库钥匙丛书

TITLE	中文书名	类别
An Analysis of Arjun Appadurai's *Modernity at Large: Cultural Dimensions of Globalization*	解析阿尔君·阿帕杜莱《消失的现代性：全球化的文化维度》	人类学
An Analysis of Claude Lévi-Strauss's *Structural Anthropology*	解析克劳德·列维-斯特劳斯《结构人类学》	人类学
An Analysis of Marcel Mauss's *The Gift*	解析马塞尔·莫斯《礼物》	人类学
An Analysis of Jared M. Diamond's *Guns, Germs, and Steel: The Fate of Human Societies*	解析贾雷德·M. 戴蒙德《枪炮、病菌与钢铁：人类社会的命运》	人类学
An Analysis of Clifford Geertz's *The Interpretation of Cultures*	解析克利福德·格尔茨《文化的解释》	人类学
An Analysis of Philippe Ariès's *Centuries of Childhood: A Social History of Family Life*	解析菲力浦·阿利埃斯《儿童的世纪：旧制度下的儿童和家庭生活》	人类学
An Analysis of W. Chan Kim & Renée Mauborgne's *Blue Ocean Strategy*	解析金伟灿 / 勒妮·莫博涅《蓝海战略》	商业
An Analysis of John P. Kotter's *Leading Change*	解析约翰·P. 科特《领导变革》	商业
An Analysis of Michael E. Porter's *Competitive Strategy: Techniques for Analyzing Industries and Competitors*	解析迈克尔·E. 波特《竞争战略：分析产业和竞争对手的技术》	商业
An Analysis of Jean Lave & Etienne Wenger's *Situated Learning: Legitimate Peripheral Participation*	解析琼·莱夫 / 艾蒂纳·温格《情境学习：合法的边缘性参与》	商业
An Analysis of Douglas McGregor's *The Human Side of Enterprise*	解析道格拉斯·麦格雷戈《企业的人性面》	商业
An Analysis of Milton Friedman's *Capitalism and Freedom*	解析米尔顿·弗里德曼《资本主义与自由》	商业
An Analysis of Ludwig von Mises's *The Theory of Money and Credit*	解析路德维希·冯·米塞斯《货币和信用理论》	经济学
An Analysis of Adam Smith's *The Wealth of Nations*	解析亚当·斯密《国富论》	经济学
An Analysis of Thomas Piketty's *Capital in the Twenty-First Century*	解析托马斯·皮凯蒂《21世纪资本论》	经济学
An Analysis of Nassim Nicholas Taleb's *The Black Swan: The Impact of the Highly Improbable*	解析纳西姆·尼古拉斯·塔勒布《黑天鹅：如何应对不可预知的未来》	经济学
An Analysis of Ha-Joon Chang's *Kicking Away the Ladder*	解析张夏准《富国陷阱：发达国家为何踢开梯子》	经济学
An Analysis of Thomas Robert Malthus's *An Essay on the Principle of Population*	解析托马斯·罗伯特·马尔萨斯《人口论》	经济学

An Analysis of John Maynard Keynes's *The General Theory of Employment, Interest and Money*	解析约翰·梅纳德·凯恩斯《就业、利息和货币通论》	经济学
An Analysis of Milton Friedman's *The Role of Monetary Policy*	解析米尔顿·弗里德曼《货币政策的作用》	经济学
An Analysis of Burton G. Malkiel's *A Random Walk Down Wall Street*	解析伯顿·G. 马尔基尔《漫步华尔街》	经济学
An Analysis of Friedrich A. Hayek's *The Road to Serfdom*	解析弗里德里希·A.哈耶克《通往奴役之路》	经济学
An Analysis of Charles P. Kindleberger's *Manias, Panics, and Crashes: A History of Financial Crises*	解析查尔斯·P.金德尔伯格《疯狂、惊恐和崩溃：金融危机史》	经济学
An Analysis of Amartya Sen's *Development as Freedom*	解析阿马蒂亚·森《以自由看待发展》	经济学
An Analysis of Rachel Carson's *Silent Spring*	解析蕾切尔·卡森《寂静的春天》	地理学
An Analysis of Charles Darwin's *On the Origin of Species: by Means of Natural Selection, or The Preservation of Favoured Races in the Struggle for Life*	解析查尔斯·达尔文《物种起源》	地理学
An Analysis of World Commission on Environment and Development's *The Brundtland Report: Our Common Future*	解析世界环境与发展委员会《布伦特兰报告：我们共同的未来》	地理学
An Analysis of James E. Lovelock's *Gaia: A New Look at Life on Earth*	解析詹姆斯·E.拉伍洛克《盖娅：地球生命的新视野》	地理学
An Analysis of Paul Kennedy's *The Rise and Fall of the Great Powers: Economic Change and Military Conflict from 1500–2000*	解析保罗·肯尼迪《大国的兴衰：1500—2000 年的经济变革与军事冲突》	历史
An Analysis of Janet L. Abu-Lughod's *Before European Hegemony: The World System A. D. 1250–1350*	解析珍妮特·L.阿布-卢格霍德《欧洲霸权之前：1250—1350 年的世界体系》	历史
An Analysis of Alfred W. Crosby's *The Columbian Exchange: Biological and Cultural Consequences of 1492*	解析艾尔弗雷德·W.克罗斯比《哥伦布大交换：1492 年以后的生物影响和文化冲击》	历史
An Analysis of Tony Judt's *Postwar: A History of Europe since 1945*	解析托尼·朱特《战后欧洲史》	历史
An Analysis of Richard J. Evans's *In Defence of History*	解析理查德·J.艾文斯《捍卫历史》	历史
An Analysis of Eric Hobsbawm's *The Age of Revolution: Europe 1789–1848*	解析艾瑞克·霍布斯鲍姆《革命的年代：欧洲 1789—1848 年》	历史

An Analysis of Roland Barthes's *Mythologies*	解析罗兰·巴特《神话学》	文学与批判理论
An Analysis of Simone de Beauvoir's *The Second Sex*	解析西蒙娜·德·波伏娃《第二性》	文学与批判理论
An Analysis of Edward W. Said's *Orientalism*	解析爱德华·W. 萨义德《东方主义》	文学与批判理论
An Analysis of Virginia Woolf's *A Room of One's Own*	解析弗吉尼亚·伍尔芙《一间自己的房间》	文学与批判理论
An Analysis of Judith Butler's *Gender Trouble*	解析朱迪斯·巴特勒《性别麻烦》	文学与批判理论
An Analysis of Ferdinand de Saussure's *Course in General Linguistics*	解析费尔迪南·德·索绪尔《普通语言学教程》	文学与批判理论
An Analysis of Susan Sontag's *On Photography*	解析苏珊·桑塔格《论摄影》	文学与批判理论
An Analysis of Walter Benjamin's *The Work of Art in the Age of Mechanical Reproduction*	解析瓦尔特·本雅明《机械复制时代的艺术作品》	文学与批判理论
An Analysis of W. E. B. Du Bois's *The Souls of Black Folk*	解析 W.E.B. 杜波依斯《黑人的灵魂》	文学与批判理论
An Analysis of Plato's *The Republic*	解析柏拉图《理想国》	哲学
An Analysis of Plato's *Symposium*	解析柏拉图《会饮篇》	哲学
An Analysis of Aristotle's *Metaphysics*	解析亚里士多德《形而上学》	哲学
An Analysis of Aristotle's *Nicomachean Ethics*	解析亚里士多德《尼各马可伦理学》	哲学
An Analysis of Immanuel Kant's *Critique of Pure Reason*	解析伊曼努尔·康德《纯粹理性批判》	哲学
An Analysis of Ludwig Wittgenstein's *Philosophical Investigations*	解析路德维希·维特根斯坦《哲学研究》	哲学
An Analysis of G. W. F. Hegel's *Phenomenology of Spirit*	解析 G.W.F. 黑格尔《精神现象学》	哲学
An Analysis of Baruch Spinoza's *Ethics*	解析巴鲁赫·斯宾诺莎《伦理学》	哲学
An Analysis of Hannah Arendt's *The Human Condition*	解析汉娜·阿伦特《人的境况》	哲学
An Analysis of G. E. M. Anscombe's *Modern Moral Philosophy*	解析 G.E.M. 安斯康姆《现代道德哲学》	哲学
An Analysis of David Hume's *An Enquiry Concerning Human Understanding*	解析大卫·休谟《人类理解研究》	哲学

An Analysis of Søren Kierkegaard's *Fear and Trembling*	解析索伦·克尔凯郭尔《恐惧与战栗》	哲学
An Analysis of René Descartes's *Meditations on First Philosophy*	解析勒内·笛卡尔《第一哲学沉思录》	哲学
An Analysis of Friedrich Nietzsche's *On the Genealogy of Morality*	解析弗里德里希·尼采《论道德的谱系》	哲学
An Analysis of Gilbert Ryle's *The Concept of Mind*	解析吉尔伯特·赖尔《心的概念》	哲学
An Analysis of Thomas Kuhn's *The Structure of Scientific Revolutions*	解析托马斯·库恩《科学革命的结构》	哲学
An Analysis of John Stuart Mill's *Utilitarianism*	解析约翰·斯图亚特·穆勒《功利主义》	哲学
An Analysis of Aristotle's *Politics*	解析亚里士多德《政治学》	政治学
An Analysis of Niccolò Machiavelli's *The Prince*	解析尼科洛·马基雅维利《君主论》	政治学
An Analysis of Karl Marx's *Capital*	解析卡尔·马克思《资本论》	政治学
An Analysis of Benedict Anderson's *Imagined Communities*	解析本尼迪克特·安德森《想象的共同体》	政治学
An Analysis of Samuel P. Huntington's *The Clash of Civilizations and the Remaking of World Order*	解析塞缪尔·P.亨廷顿《文明的冲突与世界秩序的重建》	政治学
An Analysis of Alexis de Tocqueville's *Democracy in America*	解析阿列克西·德·托克维尔《论美国的民主》	政治学
An Analysis of John A. Hobson's *Imperialism: A Study*	解析约翰·A.霍布森《帝国主义》	政治学
An Analysis of Thomas Paine's *Common Sense*	解析托马斯·潘恩《常识》	政治学
An Analysis of John Rawls's *A Theory of Justice*	解析约翰·罗尔斯《正义论》	政治学
An Analysis of Francis Fukuyama's *The End of History and the Last Man*	解析弗朗西斯·福山《历史的终结与最后的人》	政治学
An Analysis of John Locke's *Two Treatises of Government*	解析约翰·洛克《政府论》	政治学
An Analysis of Sun Tzu's *The Art of War*	解析孙武《孙子兵法》	政治学
An Analysis of Henry Kissinger's *World Order: Reflections on the Character of Nations and the Course of History*	解析亨利·基辛格《世界秩序》	政治学
An Analysis of Jean-Jacques Rousseau's *The Social Contract*	解析让-雅克·卢梭《社会契约论》	政治学

An Analysis of Odd Arne Westad's *The Global Cold War: Third World Interventions and the Making of Our Times*	解析文安立《全球冷战：美苏对第三世界的干涉与当代世界的形成》	政治学
An Analysis of Sigmund Freud's *The Interpretation of Dreams*	解析西格蒙德·弗洛伊德《梦的解析》	心理学
An Analysis of William James' *The Principles of Psychology*	解析威廉·詹姆斯《心理学原理》	心理学
An Analysis of Philip Zimbardo's *The Lucifer Effect*	解析菲利普·津巴多《路西法效应》	心理学
An Analysis of Leon Festinger's *A Theory of Cognitive Dissonance*	解析利昂·费斯汀格《认知失调论》	心理学
An Analysis of Richard H. Thaler & Cass R. Sunstein's *Nudge: Improving Decisions about Health, Wealth, and Happiness*	解析理查德·H.泰勒/卡斯·R.桑斯坦《助推：如何做出有关健康、财富和幸福的更优决策》	心理学
An Analysis of Gordon Allport's *The Nature of Prejudice*	解析高尔登·奥尔波特《偏见的本质》	心理学
An Analysis of Steven Pinker's *The Better Angels of Our Nature: Why Violence Has Declined*	解析斯蒂芬·平克《人性中的善良天使：暴力为什么会减少》	心理学
An Analysis of Stanley Milgram's *Obedience to Authority*	解析斯坦利·米尔格拉姆《对权威的服从》	心理学
An Analysis of Betty Friedan's *The Feminine Mystique*	解析贝蒂·弗里丹《女性的奥秘》	心理学
An Analysis of David Riesman's *The Lonely Crowd: A Study of the Changing American Character*	解析大卫·理斯曼《孤独的人群：美国人社会性格演变之研究》	社会学
An Analysis of Franz Boas's *Race, Language and Culture*	解析弗朗兹·博厄斯《种族、语言与文化》	社会学
An Analysis of Pierre Bourdieu's *Outline of a Theory of Practice*	解析皮埃尔·布尔迪厄《实践理论大纲》	社会学
An Analysis of Max Weber's *The Protestant Ethic and the Spirit of Capitalism*	解析马克斯·韦伯《新教伦理与资本主义精神》	社会学
An Analysis of Jane Jacobs's *The Death and Life of Great American Cities*	解析简·雅各布斯《美国大城市的死与生》	社会学
An Analysis of C. Wright Mills's *The Sociological Imagination*	解析C.赖特·米尔斯《社会学的想象力》	社会学
An Analysis of Robert E. Lucas Jr.'s *Why Doesn't Capital Flow from Rich to Poor Countries?*	解析小罗伯特·E.卢卡斯《为何资本不从富国流向穷国？》	社会学

An Analysis of Émile Durkheim's *On Suicide*	解析埃米尔·迪尔凯姆《自杀论》	社会学
An Analysis of Eric Hoffer's *The True Believer: Thoughts on the Nature of Mass Movements*	解析埃里克·霍弗《狂热分子：群众运动圣经》	社会学
An Analysis of Jared M. Diamond's *Collapse: How Societies Choose to Fail or Survive*	解析贾雷德·M.戴蒙德《大崩溃：社会如何选择兴亡》	社会学
An Analysis of Michel Foucault's *The History of Sexuality Vol. 1: The Will to Knowledge*	解析米歇尔·福柯《性史（第一卷）：求知意志》	社会学
An Analysis of Michel Foucault's *Discipline and Punish*	解析米歇尔·福柯《规训与惩罚》	社会学
An Analysis of Richard Dawkins's *The Selfish Gene*	解析理查德·道金斯《自私的基因》	社会学
An Analysis of Antonio Gramsci's *Prison Notebooks*	解析安东尼奥·葛兰西《狱中札记》	社会学
An Analysis of Augustine's *Confessions*	解析奥古斯丁《忏悔录》	神学
An Analysis of C. S. Lewis's *The Abolition of Man*	解析 C. S. 路易斯《人之废》	神学

图书在版编目（CIP）数据

解析贾雷德·M.戴蒙德《大崩溃：社会如何选择兴亡》：汉、英 / 鲁道夫·马乔（Rodolfo Maggio）著；刘露译.—上海：上海外语教育出版社，2020（世界思想宝库钥匙丛书）

ISBN 978-7-5446-6479-0

Ⅰ.①解… Ⅱ.①鲁… ②刘… Ⅲ.①社会学－研究－汉、英 Ⅳ.①C91

中国版本图书馆CIP数据核字（2020）第109936号

This Chinese-English bilingual edition of *An Analysis of Jared M. Diamond's* Collapse How Societies Choose to Fail or Survive is published by arrangement with Macat International Limited. Licensed for sale throughout the world.

本书汉英双语版由Macat国际有限公司授权上海外语教育出版社有限公司出版。供在全世界范围内发行、销售。

图字：09－2018－549

出版发行：上海外语教育出版社
　　　　　　（上海外国语大学内）　邮编：200083
电　　话：021-65425300（总机）
电子邮箱：bookinfo@sflep.com.cn
网　　址：http://www.sflep.com
责任编辑：杨莹雪

印　　刷：上海叶大印务发展有限公司
开　　本：890×1240　1/32　印张 6.25　字数 128千字
版　　次：2020年11月第1版　2020年11月第1次印刷
印　　数：2 100 册

书　　号：ISBN 978-7-5446-6479-0
定　　价：30.00 元

本版图书如有印装质量问题，可向本社调换
质量服务热线：4008-213-263　电子邮箱：editorial@sflep.com